Christian Leadership
in
Indian America

Christian Leadership in Indian America

Edited by
Tom Claus
and
Dale W. Kietzman

MOODY PRESS
CHICAGO

© 1976, by
Christian Hope Indian Eskimo
Fellowship
All rights reserved. No part of this book may be reproduced in any form without permission in writing from the publisher, except in the case of brief quotations embodied in critical articles or reviews.

Library of Congress Cataloging in Publication Data
Main entry under title:

Christian leadership in Indian America.

   Includes bibliographical references.
   1. Indians—Missions—Addresses, essays, lectures.
   2. Christian leadership—Addresses, essays, lectures.
I. Claus, Tom, 1929-   II. Kietzman, Dale.
E59.M65C46   266'.022'0973   77-9076
ISBN: 0-8024-1417-6

Printed in the United States of America

CONTENTS

Chapter	Page
Preface	7
1. A True Native Leadership *Tom Claus*	9
2. Leadership Readiness of the American Indian *Donald Johnson*	15
3. Christianity and Native American Rights *Chris C. Cavender*	29
4. The American Indian Movement and Christianity *Emile Garson*	41
5. Indian Leadership in Indian Evangelism *Billy Graham*	47
6. Christian Education in an Indian Context *Raymond G. Baines*	57
7. Working with the Indian Church *Thomas Francis, Charlie Lee, Jerry Sloan*	63
8. Developing Lay Leadership *Claudio B. Iglesias*	71
9. The Wonder World of Words *Raymond L. Gowan*	77
10. Language Problems Facing Native Americans *Randall H. Speirs*	83

11. Obstacles to Economic Development 89
    Kogee Thomas
12. Indian Rights in Latin America 99
    Dale W. Kietzman
13. Legitimate Political Aspirations 105
    Charles E. Smith
    Appendix 111
    Postscript 121

PREFACE

As a result of the thorough airing of grievances during the past several years, beginning with confrontations at Wounded Knee, all Americans have been aroused and awakened to the needs of the Native American people. Their cause is just; government officials, commercial interests, and even missionaries have been less than forthright in representing us to them.

We Christians must also carry a special burden for the spiritual needs of hundreds of thousands of Indians. Regardless of the cause and extent of their physical suffering, we should have provided the spiritual support—that encouragement of faith—they have lacked in their hour of testing.

Our responsibility—and our opportunities—are greater than ever before. Native Americans are the fastest growing segment of our population today. They need our encouragement and friendship now more than ever before. And, in spite of the history of injustice, the great majority are still open to the Gospel of Jesus Christ.

One of the most encouraging developments on the Indian scene has been the expressed desire of many mature Indian men and women to exert Christian leadership in all areas of Indian life. This fresh response to Christian responsibility is best demonstrated in the activites of CHIEF—Christian Hope Indian Eskimo Fellowship—the organization that resulted from the Albuquerque Conference on Indian Evangelism and Christian Leadership. I commend that group for your prayers and support.

The greatest moments of Indian history may lie ahead of us if a great spiritual renewal and awakening should take place.

The Indian is a sleeping giant. He is awakening. The original Americans could become the evangelists who will help win America for Christ!

BILLY GRAHAM

1

A TRUE NATIVE LEADERSHIP

Tom Claus

At a critical time and in a significant place, God brought together outstanding Native Americans for an important meeting.

Coming from all over North America, representing different races, different tribes, different cultures, and different church affiliations, we gathered in Albuquerque. We realized then, as we do now, that because of our faith in the finished work of Jesus Christ on the cross, we are one. I am convinced God is pleased when we join together as brothers and sisters in Christ to fellowship in His name.

In the book of Acts it is evident that the early church was made up of Jews, Africans, Romans, Greeks, Arabians, Egyptians, and many others. Race, tribe, culture, and class were irrelevant.

Whenever race or secondary doctrines or trivial patterns of behavior divide us, the Holy Spirit will be limited in using us for the evangelization of our Native Americans and the world. But thanks be to God, Christ transcends these differences by giving us a higher and ultimate sense of loyalty, a new center of gravitation, and a new status that makes our distinctions small and meaningless.

We hold the conviction that evangelism is the only revolutionary force that can change our world for the good. And what is evangelism? It is so to present Christ Jesus in the power of the Holy Spirit that men shall come to put their trust in God through Him, to accept Him as their King in the fellowship of His church.

What is holding back the thrust of evangelism among our Native American people—Are we mobilizing the native laity and involving them in evangelism? Are we willing to coordinate our efforts and share our information, resources, and experience as well as our problems, burdens, and mistakes— We must band together and form a spiritual "warrior society" if we are going to finish the task of evangelizing and making disciples of our people.

The unconverted Indian looks at us Evangelicals and asks, "How can their religion be right when they are so divided? Our Indian religion keeps us as one." We are so busy going in our own directions that we fail to demonstrate the oneness of the Body of Christ. In Christ's high-priestly prayer in John 17, He prayed, "That they all may be one; as thou, Father, art in me, and I in thee, that they also may be one in us: that the world may believe that thou hast sent me" (v. 21).

We are not calling for church unity but for the spiritual unity of evangelical Native American believers. What greater testimony could we give to the Indian world than the oneness we have in Christ? We are one in the Spirit. We are one in His love. We are one in the fellowship of the family of God.

It is time that we had a strong, Christian Native American voice to let the whole world know where we stand. The Lord Jesus Christ is our Chief. We have nothing to be backward

A True Native Leadership

about. He is the answer for the racial, political, economic, social, and spiritual problems we face. Let us hold our banner high and be counted. Let us unite our voices in one great swelling chorus and sing till every Indian and Eskimo hears the words, "He is Lord!"

The greatest need we have in our churches today is for native leadership. We need more educated native pastors, evangelists, and teachers. Today more than thirty thousand of our young people are in universities and colleges. We must pray for and encourage them and provide opportunities for more of them to enter Christian service.

The Lord Jesus said, "The harvest truly is plenteous, but the labourers are few; pray ye therefore the Lord of the harvest, that he will send forth labourers into his harvest" (Matthew 9:37-38).

The harvest is great. The harvest is now. Every generation is strategic. Are we going to reach our generation with the Gospel of the Lord Jesus Christ? If we do not act now and train Native American leaders, we may fall far short of completing our task. We must not fail to meet the challenge of this hour.

We must provide a biblical standard for evangelical Native Americans who are frustrated about the issue of Indian rights. The Bible has the answers.

The Gospel of our Lord Jesus Christ upholds the dignity of man by offering a recovery of his squandered destiny through forgiveness of sins and a new life. The God of the Bible is a God of justice and of justification. The Christian has a message doubly relevant to the modern scene. He knows that justice is due all because a just God created mankind in His holy image, and he knows that all men need justification. The Gospel is Good News not simply because it reinforces modern man's sense of personal worth and confirms the demand for universal justice on the basis of creation, but also because it offers the doomed sinner justification and redemption through the Lord Jesus Christ.

We have lost our Indian rights because of man's sin. Sin is the real issue. The world is filled with injustice because man's heart is filled with sin. And sin can be removed only by the blood of the Lord Jesus Christ. We must pray for a spiritual awakening in our country, among our national and state leaders, so they will seek the face of the Lord and do what is right and just for the Native American.

Even though we must defend the rights of our Native American people, as Christians we must do it in the spirit of Christ. "For though we walk in the flesh, we do not war after the flesh: (for the weapons of our warfare are not carnal, but mighty through God to the pulling down of strong holds;)" (2 Cor 10:3-4).

This is a critical time because we can no longer evade these issues. We must set objectives and take new directions in our ministry to our people if we are going to achieve our goals in evangelism, education, and Christian leadership.

1. We need to develop a strong and growing lay leadership within tribal communities through encouraging small Bible study groups, extension seminaries, and lay leadership programs.
2. We need to provide fellowship for evangelical Indian Christians, information about the international Christian Indian scene, and a legitimate Indian voice to the whole Church, to the non-Church public, and to governments on issues that concern us.
3. We need to survey the possibility for an international Indian congress on evangelism in the near future, with

A True Native Leadership

Indian pastors, evangelists, and Christian leaders participating from the entire Western world.
4. We need to encourage more qualified Indian young people to go on to higher education through scholarship programs, and to work toward a Christian Indian institution of higher education built around a seminary program.
5. We need to create pride in Indian identity, native abilities, and leadership potential through the recognition of outstanding achievement and innovative leadership. I suggest this can be achieved principally through a new Christian periodical designed solely for Native Americans.
6. We need to acquaint the Church at large with those programs and organizations that make a distinctive evangelical contribution to Indian communities and churches, and we need to mobilize the Church to a greater degree to stand behind effective evangelical causes.

By what method can these objectives be reached? I propose an international fellowship of Indians and Eskimo and their friends who are concerned for the development of indigenous Christian leadership among native communities. This organization should include our South and Central American Indian brethren, too. This fellowship would be an Indian National Association of Evangelicals. It would seek to coordinate and utilize existing programs, personnel, and facilities and not seek to have its own large staff and facilities. It would endeavor to sharpen the focus of all of us on effective means of achieving a true native leadership and sense of Christian mission.

Let us begin a movement for God that will touch every

Native American in our generation. Let us not limit God in His working, and let us not fail to be ready for a new and great outpouring of the Holy Spirit in this critical period of history. Our spiritual resources are unlimited. God works through human vessels that are dedicated and yielded to Him. God wants to work through you and me. Will we let Him do His perfect work in us, in our cities, reservations, and villages? If we will, we could change our world.

2

LEADERSHIP READINESS OF THE AMERICAN INDIAN

Donald Johnson

A few years ago a friend of mine who traces his ancestry to an Indian tribe located in the southern part of the United States was in the hospital. While I was visiting him, the head nurse came in to explain the rules of visitation. When I excused myself briefly, she turned to my friend and asked him if he was an Indian. His barely audible reply was "Uh, no. I am Spanish."

The reason my friend and other Indian people deny their ancestry in certain situations clearly reflects the fact that Indian people have so often been considered and treated as inferiors.

Historically, Indian people had a healthy regard for their own being and way of life. Benjamin Franklin wrote in 1784:

This paper is adapted from a chapter of the author's thesis written to fulfill the requirements for the Master of Divinity degree at Concordia Theological Seminary, Springfield, Illinois. The insights and observations come from three months of travel visiting reservations and Indian communities throughout the Southwest.

> Savages we call them, because their manners differ from ours, which we think the perfection of civility; they think the same of theirs. . . . Our laborious manner of life, compared with theirs, they esteem slavish and base, and the learning, on which we value ourselves, they regard as frivolous and useless.

At first, Indians tended to view the white man as inferior. Schooled in practical survival skills, Indians were amazed that the white man was so helpless and unskilled.

Nevertheless, in view of the sheer numbers of Europeans coming to the Americas, inevitably what Indians considered important and what they valued had to be surrendered to the dominant peoples. Perhaps no alteration in man's adaptation to life on this earth had ever been achieved on so vast a scale. In the span of a lifetime, a continent was jerked through five thousand years of man's history. To the Indians, so recently its sole human occupants, it was more than a change or a defeat; it was the end of their Indian world.

In this "end of his world," the Indian surrendered much more than his land and his culture. He surrendered his self-concept, his own personal judgment of his worthiness. Surroundings that provide love, care, opportunity to succeed, and tangible social recognition generally provide the best environment for the development of a healthy self-concept.

Conversely, an impoverished home environment and lack of social recognition contribute toward a poor self-concept. Within the context of this understanding of human personality development, we can understand the Indian experience.

Before the coming of the white man, the Indian had developed a life-style that was quite different from that of the

Leadership Readiness of the American Indian

European peoples. The Indian people of that time emphasized individualism in contrast to the European concept of government supremacy. This individualism was balanced in Indian tribes by long-established customs and experience, which provided the direction and cohesiveness necessary to maintain their societies.

When European peoples came to America, they immediately attempted to subject the Indian people to a form of government alien to their culture. This disrupted the Indian's view of himself, since it destroyed the basic standard by which he measured his self-worth.

Add to this the seizure of the traditional Indian lands, the destruction of the buffalo, and the directed efforts to change Indian culture, and you can begin to understand how the Indian self-concept could be greatly affected.

Satanta, one of the great chiefs of the Kiowa, in addressing a congressional peace commission in 1867, provided us with a view of Indian concern for maintaining their own way of life:

> All the land south of the Arkansas belongs to the Kiowas and Comanches, and I don't want to give away any of it. I love the land and the buffalo and will not part with it. I want you to understand well what I say.... I want the children raised as I was. When I make peace, it is a long and lasting one—there is no end to it.... I have heard that you intend to settle us on a reservation near the mountains. I don't want to settle. I love to roam over the prairies. There I feel free and happy, but when we settle down we grow pale and die.

At that same peace commission, Ten Bears of the Comanches said:

> I was born on the prairie, where the wind blew free, and there was nothing to break the light of the sun. I was born

where there were no enclosures, and where everything drew a free breath. I want to die there and not within walls. I knew every stream and every wood between the Rio Grande and the Arkansas. I have hunted and lived over that great country. I lived like my fathers before me and, like them, I lived happily....

The Texans have taken away the places where the grass grew the thickest and the timber was the best. Had we kept that, we might have done the thing you ask. But it is too late. The white man has the country which we loved and we only wish to wander on the prairie until we die. I want no blood upon my land to stain the grass. I want it all clear and pure, and I wish it so, that all who go through among my people may find peace when they come in, and leave it when they go out.

Paul Tournier, in the introduction to chapter 2 of *A Place for You*, writes:

> Man needs a place, and this need is vital to him. Where, then, does the need come from? I believe that in fact it is a manifestation of a need to live, to exist, to have a place in life. Life is not an abstraction. To exist is to occupy a particular living-space to which one has a right. This is true even of animals. The zoologist, Professor Portmann, of Basle, pointed out to me that the seagulls on the railings along the quay-side always stand at least twelve inches apart. If another gull comes down between them, they fly away at once. All respect the law, that each has a right to a minimum living space.[1]

Tournier further maintains that this seeking for a place goes beyond a simple searching for a physical location. It manifests itself in the desire of each person to be loved and appreciated. A withholding of love and appreciation, there-

---

1. Paul Tournier, *A Place for You*, (New York: Harper & Row, 1968), p. 25.

Leadership Readiness of the American Indian

fore, is essentially a deprivation of place. Deprivation of love and deprivation of place overlap.

Applying this understanding of human experience to the Indian people, we can begin to see that the concept of Indian inferiority, the annihilation of Indian tribes, the destruction of cultures and tribal societies, and the seizure of Indian lands were essentially a deprivation of love. It was a denial of the principle "that each has a right to a minimum living space."

Though the Indian people probably did not fully understand the psychological processes involved in the destruction of their self-concept, they were nevertheless well aware that their personalities were being disastrously altered. Black Hawk, of the Sauk tribe, addressed his people in 1832:

> Headmen, chiefs, braves and warriors of the Sauks: For more than a hundred winters our nation was a powerful, happy and united people.... Our children were never known to cry of hunger, and no stranger, red or white, was permitted to enter our lodges without finding food and rest. Our nation was respected by all who came in contact with it, for we had the ability as well as the courage to defend and maintain our rights of territory, person and property against the world. Then, indeed, was it an honor to be called a Sauk, for that name was a passport to our people traveling in other territories and among other nations. But an evil day befell us when we became a divided nation, and with that division our glory deserted us, leaving us with the hearts and heels of the rabbit in place of the courage and strength of the bear.

One might rationalize that the psychological and spiritual decay of Indian nations in the days of colonial America and the later settlement of the old West was evidence of their innate inferiority. However, recent studies of human behavior have shown that deprivation of love and self-worth, such as that experienced by Indian people, is associated with delinquency, loneliness, neuroses, and other dysfunctional behavior in all peoples.

The Indian people experienced a human tragedy, and in their despair and defeat they passed on their frustrations to their children. This cycle has continued from generation to generation until the present day, a phenomenon that is not unique to the Indian experience.

Charles F. Kemp, writing about America's present-day poor, noted that poverty can twist and deform the spirit. It is destructive to both aspiration and hope. The hopelessness of the parents is passed on to the children from generation to generation.

This transforms the past experiences of Indian people into present reality. Even though Indians today may be totally unfamiliar with the tragic history of their people, they are still the unfortunate victims of that past.

They move from reservations to the city, only to discover they should have stayed on the reservation. They are lost in the city, unhealthy and unhappy.

In a conversation with an Indian mother several years ago, I asked, "If you really love your children, how can you allow your house to become so messy and then go out and drink?"

She replied angrily, "You have no business asking me that. Who do you think you are? You are no good. I hate my children! They come between me and my husband. I hate them! I hate God." She used curse words against God. "He is no good. He doesn't care."

A pause followed, and then she cried. "You are right. I can't love my children. I have never learned to love. Neither have my brothers and sisters. Ever since we were small, our

Leadership Readiness of the American Indian

parents fought and drank. And whenever they did, we had to find someone to stay with. We went from house to house. I cannot love because I have never experienced love."

In essence, that deprivation of love, which had been so destructive in the history of her people, was now creating havoc in her own life and in the lives of her children. Her strong response to the stress was to give an appearance of assurance and aggressiveness in order to hide her weakness and to cover up her own fear.

This fear engendered by stress tends to keep Indians from going on to greater accomplishments. The president of an Indian Bible school, himself an Indian, made these observations in a private interview with me about his Indian students, many of whom came long distances from various tribes to attend the school:

> I noticed a spirit of shyness, a lack of desire to be leaders, unsureness of themselves. We have that in a majority of students who come. Very few are really outgoing and can cope with the situation here on their own. I think this is true wherever we go with our Indian people. I think that the Indian people right here in this community alone have been put down. They have been told time and again that they can't do it. And now they believe it. As a result, it is difficult to really get them into the leadership. For so long they've been told that they were more or less second-class citizens—they were not equal to the non-Indian. And I know this to be a fact right here, so that when an Indian person is in line for a promotion or seeking a better job, the reaction is, "What is he trying to prove?" This is a reaction of the non-Indians.

Fear of being judged harshly by the white community often prevents the Indian from going on. But, says this Bible school president, there is also a fear of being judged harshly by the Indian community:

There is some of this very thing in the Indians themselves. I have seen it right in our own public school, in our own high school, when there is a mixed chorus or a band program. We have tried for years to get our Indian kids involved in this kind of thing. The Indian kids sit up front and make fun of their own Indian friends: "They shouldn't be up there. What are they doing?" I have seen the kids in the program distracted and discouraged to the point where they won't even come out for chorus and this kind of thing. So it is not only from the non-Indians, but it is from their own Indian peers, their own friends.

The students who refused to try out for band or glee club for fear of offending their peer group were responding in weakness. In turning out for band, they risked ridicule and the accusation that they were becoming like whites. Participation had become a threat to their self-concept.

The Indian students who aggressively ridiculed fellow students participating in the band were also acting in fear. They were afraid that the success of certain Indians from among their peer group would cause them embarrassment. Too often they have been told that a good Indian is the one who becomes as much like middle-class America as possible.

It is not surprising, then, that the term *apple Indian* has developed. This derogatory term is usually applied to Indian people who have become like white people. As an apple is red on the outside and white on the inside, the Indian who identifies himself too much with white people is no longer a true Indian. He is red on the outside, but down deep in his heart he is white. This term is really a defense mechanism, an aggressive reaction to cover up personal fears and weaknesses.

A leader of the American Indian Movement, who had been in and out of jail as a drunk and junkie, says, "When I found out that as an Indian I was in fact among the most beautiful people in the Western hemisphere, that's when I got off skid row. That's when I finished college."

The American Indian Movement (AIM) often emphasizes the virtues of the Indian way as opposed to the ways of the white man. The Church therefore, is one of its favorite targets. As far as AIM is concerned, the Church is not only an agency of the white man's domination of the American Indian, but it is also foreign to the Indian way. The more radical elements of the movement have threatened to close churches, and the pastors on Indian reservations are naturally quite concerned.

Christian churches are going to have to listen carefully to the concerns expressed by such organizations, since they do offer insights into Indian grievances that otherwise might not be heard. The Church also must become sensitive to this interplay of the strong and the weak, recognizing that fear is often basic to the reactions of Indian people. They are afraid of so many things; their lives have been influenced by so many forces, hurt in so many ways.

The Church must also recognize the Gospel message as the key to reaching out to the Indian. Through the Gospel, man finds his real worth as a child of God. The Reverend Bill Frague, a Pueblo Indian from New Mexico, points us in the proper direction:

> We Indians have a big problem, especially out here in the Southwest. The principal problems are alcohol, suicide, divorce, family abandonment, neglect—all of these things which bring hardship to families and loved ones. As ministers of the Gospel, I believe we can introduce these people to the Lord Jesus Christ, the Christ of all crises. Not just talking about Him, reading about Him, or hearing about Him, but leading them in a way so that Christ will become

real in their lives. Jesus, when He becomes real in a person's life, changes that person; he is a new creature in Christ. He begins to realize his responsibility. He begins to hold his head up. And he begins to be more concerned about how he lives wherever he goes.

In the Scriptures, the weak are lifted up and made strong by the power of God. The strong are broken and made to realize their weakness. Then they are made truly strong by the same power of God. Paul writes to the Corinthian Christians: "For consider your calling, brethren, that there were not many wise according to the flesh, not many mighty, not many noble; but God has chosen the foolish things of the world to shame the wise, and God has chosen the weak things of the world to shame the things which are strong" (1 Cor 1:26-27, NASB).

As great as the psychological and emotional impact of white colonization and settlement was on the American Indian, the effect on his spiritual development was even more devastating. The Christians of colonial America often viewed the Indian people as children of the devil. Indian religious ceremonies and rites were considered demonic activity. In some instances, the Indian religions were devoid of a hope of eternal life. One Navajo Indian described to me the Navajo view of life beyond the grave in this way:

> When a person died, the spirit would leave his body and then dwell right in the area where the body was buried. There was a great fear. It is a religion that brought fear, and I feared to die. I feared death, and there was never any answer when you inquired about life hereafter. You were told just not to talk about it; it was taboo. You would bring misfortune upon your family.

Seen from this perspective, one might conclude that Christianity offered a refreshing change from some of the

Indian concepts of God and the hereafter. To many Indian people, who by God's grace have experienced the rebirth, it has been that. Note the testimony of a Cheyenne Indian:

> My dad wouldn't listen to anybody. He said that the Bible is only for the white man. Christ is only for the white man. He is not for us. This Bible came from across the sea. It cannot be for us. Here is our own. The peyote is for us. It is for the Indian people. My dad became a Christian. And now you can't convince him that the Bible is only for the white man, that Christ is only for the white man. He said, "Those were my arguments before I came face to face with Him, before I experienced what He could do."
>
> When I was still in Japan, I received a letter from my folks. They said, "We have some wonderful news for you when you come home." And I said to myself, "Huh! Some rich relatives have died. They must have a whole bunch of money." I came home, got off the bus, and here they came after me. They took me straight home. I had come home sick. Then it dawned on me what this great news was—that Dad was a Christian! And to me this was great news. This was better to me than anything in my life. For that is what the white man has brought to us—the Christ! I am convinced that this was all in the plan of God, that the white man should bring us to Christ, so that we, the Indian people, could also learn of His plan of salvation—and that it also includes us.

For the large number of Indian people who did not experience Christian rebirth, the coming of Christianity and civilization set the stage for a plunge into a depth of spiritual depravity they had not previously known. This condition occurred because the efforts to "civilize" Indian people often involved the destruction of existing Indian religious beliefs.

The destruction of Indian religious beliefs took many different forms, sometimes violent and often very effective.

The loss of their religious beliefs introduced this subtle syllogism into Indian thinking:
1. A faithful, loving Great Spirit protects his people.
2. The Great Spirit has not protected us from all of our troubles.
3. Therefore, we cannot trust him, for he has abandoned us.

We recall the words of Chief Seattle: "Our God, the Great Spirit, seems also to have forsaken us."

The Indian people were left in a tragic spiritual position. They could no longer trust the Great Spirit, and they would not trust the white man's Christian God. They found themselves in a religious vacuum, a spiritual void.

Jesus used three arguments to refute the accusation that He did His miracles through the help of Satan. The last of them is recorded in Luke 11:21-26 (NASB):

> When a strong man fully armed guards his own homestead, his possessions are undisturbed; but when someone stronger than he attacks him and overpowers him, he takes away from him all his armor on which he had relied, and distributes his plunder. He who is not with Me is against Me; and he who does not gather with Me, scatters. When the unclean spirit goes out of a man, it passes through waterless places seeking rest, and not finding any, it says, "I will return to my house from which I came." And when it comes, it finds it swept and put in order. Then it goes and takes along seven other spirits more evil than itself, and they go in and live there; and the last state of that man becomes worse than the first.

This passage contains a strong warning against spiritual laxness. The person who is confronted with Christ must respond in true repentance and faith and not with mere passing interest. Through the preaching of John the Baptist

Leadership Readiness of the American Indian

and of Christ Himself, a new day had dawned for Israel, and the message of the Kingdom had been greeted with much enthusiasm. But the Jewish nation as such had not repented and accepted the Gospel, and the condition of unbelief into which it fell was worse than the former one had been.

In one sense, the experiences of the Jewish people and of the American Indian with regard to the Christian message are similar. In the main, both have rejected it, and both have reaped a bitter spiritual harvest. The Jews, however, still have their traditional religion to hold to, whereas the Indian people have, in many instances, been left in a complete religious void. How true is Jesus' statement that the demons "go in and live there; and the last state of that man becomes worse than the first."

Demonic influences have wreaked havoc in the lives of Indian people. Alcoholism, despair, frustration, and suicides are a tragic part of Indian communities today. On the other hand, the Scriptures also teach that Satan is the "deceiver of the nations" (see Rev 12:9). Is it not possible that this deceiver has controlled the actions of our nation at many times, in its history of Indian relations, to accomplish the spiritual destruction not only of the Indian people but also of those who have been the instruments of these destructive policies?

3

Christianity and Native American Rights

Chris C. Cavender

What should be the Native American Christian's perspective on Native American rights? This question poses a dilemma in the minds of many Native American Christians, that is, a conflict between loyalty to one's tribal heritage and tradition, and loyalty to Christianity. This question cannot be answered in a vacuum. Other factors need to be considered in attempting to formulate a position on Native American rights. The most important of these are treaties, the Judeo-Christian tradition, the evangelical imperative, and the issues raised by Vine Deloria, Jr.

What are treaties? Who is involved in making treaties? Why were treaties made? What kinds of rights emerged or were guaranteed by these treaties? Are these treaties being honored? If not, who has broken their promises?

Vine Deloria, Jr. has accurately assessed the feelings of the majority of Native Americans by declaring that the United States government has failed to honor its solemn treaty obligations. Note this passage from *Custer Died for Your Sins:*

After Lyndon B. Johnson had been elected he came before the American people with his message on Vietnam. The import of the message was that America had to keep her commitments in southeast Asia or the world would lose faith in the promises of our country.

Some years back Richard Nixon warned the American people that Russia was bad because she had not kept any treaty or agreement signed by her. You can trust the Communists, the saying went, to be Communists.

Indian people laugh themselves sick when they hear these statements. America has yet to keep one Indian treaty or agreement despite the fact that the United States government signed over four hundred such treaties and agreements with Indian tribes. It would take Russia another century to make and break as many treaties as the United States has already violated.[1]

What is a treaty? A treaty is an agreement, a contract in writing between two or more political authorities. For our purposes, it is a contract between the various Native American nations and the United States government. These treaties were, in the main, land cessions. In return, the Native American groups would be guaranteed hunting and fishing rights, ownership of their remaining lands, and other rights.

Treaties are, for the most part, still in force and are of recognized validity.[2] Some claim that treaties are a thing of the past and should not even enter into any issue or controversy regarding Native American rights. One example is Charlie McBride, who founded the White American Movement as a reaction to the takeover of the Alexian Brothers' novitiate at Gresham, Wisconsin, by the Menominee Warrior Society.

The notion that treaties have no legal effect today springs

---
1. Vine Deloria, Jr., *Custer Died for Your Sins* (New York: Avon, 1969), p. 35.
2. Nathan R. Margold, "Introduction," in Felix S. Cohen, *Handbook of Federal Indian Law* (Albuquerque: U. New Mexico, 1943), p. xxii.

Christianity and Native American Rights

from the assumption that when treaty-making was discontinued by the Indian Appropriation Act of 1871, the force of treaties in existence at that time also disappeared. This assumption is totally false. The act in question specifically stated that there was to be no lessening of obligations already incurred. These treaties made by the United States government and Native American nations are still in force and should be enforced.

Treaties between Native Amercans and the United States are not different from treaties with foreign nations. This view has been repeatedly confirmed by the federal courts and never successfully challenged.[3] The case of *Turner v. American Baptist Missionary Union* (1852), illustrates this point well. In this case the Circuit Court for the Michigan District said:

> It is contended that a treaty with Indian tribes has not the same dignity or effect as a treaty with a foreign and independent nation. This distinction is not authorized by the Constitution. Since the commencement of the government, treaties have been made with Indians, and the treaty-making power has been exercised in making them. They are treaties, within the meaning of the Constitution and, as such, are the supreme law of the land.

Another example would be *United States v. Forty-three Gallons of Whiskey* (1876), in which the Supreme Court said, with reference to the provisions of an Indian treaty:

> The Constitution declares a treaty to be the supreme law of the land; and Chief Justice Marshall, in *Foster and Elam v. Neilson*, 2 Pet. 314, has said, "That a treaty is to be regarded, in courts of justice, as equivalent to an act of the legislature, whenever it operates of itself, without the aid of any legislative provision."

---

3. Ibid., p. 33.

The essential point is that Native American rights guaranteed by treaties are being violated today. One needs only to look at the Wounded Knee trials and the Treaty of 1868; the situation at Sisseton, South Dakota; the turmoil at the Leech Lake Ojibwe Reservation in Minnesota; and the fishing rights controversy in the Northwest, which involves tribes such as the Yakima.

Various white groups—such as snowmobilers, concerned citizens committees, and sportsmen's groups—are attacking the treaty rights of Native Americans. They do it in the name of defending property rights, or in the name of conservation, or preserving the ecological balance, or equal rights for all citizens, or uniform application of civil and criminal law to all citizens, or other equally altruistic and idealistic causes.

In summary, treaties made with Native Americans are still in force. They are like treaties made with foreign nations. They are part of the supreme law of the land. And they are being violated today. Native American rights, guaranteed by treaties, make up one important factor to be considered in determining the position of the Native American Christian in regard to treaty rights. But equally important is the question of what position the Christian Church—especially the fundamental and evangelical branches—should assume with regard to the whole issue of treaty rights.

Specific aspects of the Judeo-Christian tradition must be examined in order to assess properly its influence upon an Indian Christian's viewpoint toward Native American rights. These are the cursed-land idea, the tilling-of-the-soil lifestyle, the promised-land concept, the dominion-over-nature idea, and the white-superiority connotation.

In Genesis 3:17, God cursed the earth because Eve and Adam had eaten of the forbidden fruit.

Christianity and Native American Rights

Thus, the idea of the earth and nature being corrupted is promoted. Various verses in Romans (8: 19-23) and Revelation (21: 4; 22: 3) seem to support this idea.

How different the cursed-land concept is from the attitude many Native American tribes hold toward the land. For example, among the Dakota, the word *ina*, which is applied to the land, is translated "mother." All the emotional connotations, such as affection, love, and respect, that can be derived from a relationship between a mother and her child apply to the relationship between the Dakota and the land, at least historically.

The Taos Pueblo believe that Mother Earth is pregnant in the spring, and therefore they wear soft-soled shoes and take off the shoes from the horses' hooves so that they will not hurt their mother. Other Native American groups are horrified when they see the white man plowing up the earth with his steel plows, because they feel that Mother Earth's breasts are being ripped open.

When a person feels that someone or something is bad, he finds it easier to do bad things to that someone or something. In other words, it is not surprising to an Indian that European man has plowed, cut, sawed, strip-mined, destroyed, polluted, and, in general, raped the natural resources of the North American continent. Could it be that this cursed-land concept has influenced European man's attitude toward nature?

The tilling-of-the-soil concept is also derived from the book of Genesis (3: 23). After Adam and Eve had eaten of the forbidden fruit, God banished man, His creation, from the Garden of Eden "to till the ground from whence he was taken." Man was now to eat by the sweat of his brow and by tilling the soil. Farming was a divinely ordained activity.

European man used this concept as a partial justification

for taking the Native American's land. Viewing the Native American man as a hunter, a nomad, and a beast of the forest, he felt justified in taking the land. After all, he would put the land to a better use; he would farm it. He claimed this even while burning settled communities and while stealing grain from the storehouses of the Native Americans.

It is interesting to note that one of the four major areas of plant domestication in the Americas during the time when man the hunter and fisherman became man the farmer as well was the eastern area of what is now the United States.[4] And this was Native American man several thousand years before the white man arrived. Also, it was the Indians who kept the colonists from starving those first hard winters at Jamestown and at Plymouth. The Indians taught the Europeans how to use fertilizer and how to become more efficient farmers.

Various laws in the United States were predicated upon the notion that Indians were not farmers. The act of March 3, 1819, for example, was for the purpose of civilizing the Native Americans by instructing them "in the modes of agriculture." Another extremely important act designed to make the Native American like the white farmer was the Dawes Act of 1887.

Another aspect of the Judeo-Christian tradition was the promised-land and chosen-people notion. This idea also comes from the book of Genesis (12:1; 13:14-15; 15: 18-21; 17: 8), where God makes a covenant with Abraham. The early white settlers, especially the English, felt it was their sacred duty to root out the godless Canaanites (i.e., the various Native American nations) and possess the land.

The dominion-over-nature concept is also part of the psyche of European man and comes from the Judeo-

---

4. John F. Plummer, *College Level Anthropology* (New York: Monarch, 1965), p. 87.

Christianity and Native American Rights   35

Christian tradition (see Psalm 8: 6). Man's mastery over nature is clearly taught from the Scriptures. How different this is from the attitude of most tribal religions regarding nature! Tribal man believes that man is one with nature and should live in harmony with nature. In fact, some groups feel a strong kinship with nature, referring to the fish, the birds, and the animals as brothers and sisters.

One last comment concerns the connotation of white superiority that can be found in the Scriptures. For example, John 3:19 seems to equate darkness with evil and light with good. Other verses speak of scarlet sins being made as "white as snow" (Isa 1:18) or "whiter than snow" (Psalm 51:7). It appears that the color white is suggestive of the good and the positive, while black is associated with the negative.

It is good for Native American Christians to face squarely the fact that the "Good Book" has been falsely used to teach many bad things. In some measure this has contributed to the attitudes and actions of European man toward Native American man historically, with some attitudes persisting to this day.

What is the evangelical imperative? It begins with Jesus Christ, who in John 14: 6 says, "I am the way, the truth, and the life: no man cometh unto the Father, but by me." It continues with Matthew 28:19-20, "Go ye therefore, and teach all nations, baptizing them in the name of the Father, and of the Son, and of the Holy Ghost."

The underlying assertion of this evangelical imperative is that Christianity has the truth. It is the true faith. Therefore, everybody who does not have Christianity does not have the truth and is not saved but is condemned. If people want to have the true religion, they must embrace Christianity.

This particular point is perhaps the most trying, the most

taxing, to the Native American. He wants to be loyal to Christianity and still be loyal to his own tribal heritage and tradition. Questions raised by this imperative are: What does this do to tribal cultures deeply entwined with religions that have been practiced for thousands of years before the white man ever arrived on the scene? What does this do to tribal theological systems developed thousands of years before Christ was even born?[5]

These are hard questions, but they must be confronted. They most certainly relate to the concerns and issues of Native Americans as they begin to assert themselves. For Native American Christians and for the Christian Church to ignore these questions would be folly.

The book *God Is Red* by Vine Deloria, Jr. calls for a new religious order based on Native American thought and theology. At the same time, it gives a scathing indictment of Christianity:

> What we are more interested in, however, is what effect in practical terms the various sequences of the Christian life—from initial conversion to eventual salvation—have on individuals and societies. What peculiarly distinguishes a Christian from any other person is difficult to determine. The track record of individual Christians and Christian nations is not so spectacular as to warrant anyone seriously considering becoming a Christian.
>
> Where the cross goes, there is never life more abundantly—only death, destruction and ultimately, betrayal.[6]

In *Custer Died for Your Sins*, Deloria comments with biting wit and penetrating insight on various aspects of the

---
5. Edward H. Spicer, *A Short History of the Indians of the United States* (New York: Van Nostrand Reinhold, 1969), pp. 262-65.
6. Vine Deloria, Jr., *God is Red* (New York: Grosset & Dunlap, 1973), pp. 194, 282.

Christianity and Native American Rights

Native American situation in contemporary society. In his section on religion and missionaries, Deloria makes a number of statements which raise issues for today's Native American Christian and for the Christian Church. Examples are:

> Indian religion appears to many of us as the only ultimate salvation for the Indian people.
>
> The best thing that the national denomination could do to ensure the revitalization of Christian missions among Indian people would be to assist in the creation of a national Indian Christian church.
>
> Younger Indians are finding in Indian nationalism and tribal religions sufficient meaning to continue their drift away from the established churches....
>
> Many denominations are skeptical about letting Indians enter the ministry because of the possibility that doctrine may become impure.
>
> No other field of endeavor in America today has as much blatant racial discrimination as does the field of Christian missions to the American Indian people.

We have discussed some factors which must be considered in deciding what the Christian Native American's viewpoint on Native American rights should be. We have also pointed out factors which contribute to a conflict in the hearts and minds of Native American Christians, namely, loyalty to Christianity versus loyalty to tribal heritage and tradition. Can we avoid the extremes?

One extreme would be a complete rejection of Christianity and Christ. Persons going this far would say that Christianity is a white man's religion. They would also say, "Look at what has happened to the Native American in the name of Christ and Christianity. Christianity has contributed to the assimilation process, the removal process, the suppression of tribal religions, the dividing up of the reservations for various denominations, the allotment policy which resulted in a loss of millions of acres of Native American lands, the notion of racial inferiority of Native Americans, and so on. We want no part of Christ or Christianity."

As a matter of fact, many Native American youth in their search for identity and in their growing nationalism are saying exactly that.

The other extreme would be the complete acceptance of Christianity and the disregard, if not rejection, of the Native American heritage and tradition. This extreme would say, "I will follow Christ no matter what. Tribal religions are paganism; therefore, one should forsake all tribal ways."

The task of the Christian Church and the Native American Christian is to find the right path. On the one hand, it must satisfy the demands of Christ (but not necessarily the Western church). On the other hand, it should retain a measure of identity and tribal integrity.

Perhaps the Church has the most to change. To what extent is the Church willing to reexamine and reevaluate its present philosophy and position regarding the Native Americans? How much is the Church willing to change in order to become more sensitive to Native American groups? How willing is the Church to find the commonalities between Christian thought and tribal religious thought? How willing is the Church to support the principle of self-determination for Native Americans in all areas, including religious worship?

For the Native American Christian, there should be no controversy regarding his position on Native American rights, for these rights have been guaranteed by treaties.

Christianity and Native American Rights

The Native American Christian can support them in good conscience.

He must make himself informed, however, especially in regard to treaties and his own tribal group. He must inform others and make them aware of how treaty rights are now being violated. And he must prick the conscience of the Church on the issue of treaty rights.

If the Church is to gain ground—spiritually, not physically—among Native American communities, it must meet these issues in a manner that is satisfactory and meaningful to Native Americans. The Church must certainly take a strong, assertive, and positive position on treaty rights. Only then will Christianity regain some of the credibility it has lost over the past four and a half centuries.

4

The American Indian Movement and Christianity

Emile Garson

The American Indian Movement (AIM) was formed in Minneapolis, Minnesota by Dennis Banks, George Mitchell, and others in an attempt to establish a feeling of community—a sense of identity through cultural activities among the Indian population. The formation of AIM was an outgrowth of the human rights and cultural awareness movement of the sixties and seventies.

Today the mass media reports the political activities of AIM almost exclusively. This type of reporting has done an injustice to its image, for it has reduced AIM to personalities. Hearing of AIM in the media only in terms of its vocal members, the public may dismiss AIM as the discontent of a few who are bent on violence. This gross oversight is an injustice. Such an erroneous judgment may hinder the Christian's understanding of the Indian situation and seriously undermine his witness to Indians.

AIM is a modern-day pan-Indian[1] movement which

---

1. Hazel W. Hertzberg (*The Search for an American Indian Identity: Modern Pan-Indian Movements* [Ithaca, N.Y.: Syracuse U., 1971]) associates pan-Indianism with identity crisis, alienation, and marginality, a view with which I agree.

places paramount importance on rights—especially land rights. Russell Means in *Akwesasne Notes* states that AIM is a liberation organization based upon the religious teachings of the old people and the ancestors, which justifies the pursuit of sovereign rights and international relationships.[2] At this point, AIM and biblical Christianity can establish a meaningful dialogue.

Jesus Christ, the Son of God, is the foremost protagonist of liberation because His death at Calvary overcame the alienation, the identity crisis, and the marginality of man. Man, because of sin, is alienated— cut off—from God. Sin prevents him from assuming his true humanity (the identity crisis) and causes certain men to live a marginal existence (in terms of property) because of man's inherent selfishness and callousness.

The liberation offered by AIM is based on the quest to reclaim usurped Indian land and to revive Indian religion and culture. AIM is considered by its adherents to be a spiritual movement, for it is aiming at religious rebirth (revival of sacred customs and practices), eventually leading to a rebirth of Indian dignity. It is also political in its demands for reclaiming Indian land, but most supporters will vow that AIM is based on religious values.

The liberation embraced by AIM is achieved by human effort. AIM does not seek out the root cause of social, economic, and political injustice, which is sin. The reclaiming of land does not address the reason for the identity problem; that is, that man is out of tune with God.

AIM adherents ascribe to the Mother Earth concept—the ground is our mother because we came from the ground and to it we will return. This pantheistic perspective contains the notion that identity is found by submerging the indi-

---

2. Russell Means, quoted in *Akwesasne Notes* 6 (January 1975), no. 5, p. 5.

vidual self into "the sum total of all other individual things," says Udo Middlemann in *Pro-existence*.[3] In other words, man is brother to all creation and, therefore, all things are equal. Land, being the mother, is therefore not marketable. Land is a gift for the use and enjoyment of man. However, Darcy McNickle in *Native American Tribalism*[4] points out that "individual right and use was recognized and protected."

There is no such thing as an Indian culture or religion *per se*. There are Indian cultures and religions which are functioning, adaptive mechanisms in given points of time and space. To return to the past is, therefore, analogous to returning to the horse and buggy. Culture and religion have meaning to a given people at a given point in time and space. The cultures and religions of the past cannot function in the present day because the environment and world view of peoples have changed.

To advocate a return, therefore, is not liberation but a form of slavery and idolatry to the past. Religious rebirth, in terms of the revival of past sacred customs and practices, is a facade which induces a deepening identity crisis instead of the desired rebirth of Indian dignity.

What can Christianity offer as an alternative?

The history of Indian missions has been overshadowed by failure because of two related facts: The human dignity of the Indian was not respected, and missionaries often preached their own culture as part and parcel of the message of Christ. Up to the present, Indians have continually rejected culturalized Christianity rather than Christ Himself. Culturalized Christianity presents another form of identity crisis.

---

3. Udo Middlemann, *Pro-existence* (Downers Grove, Ill.: Inter-Varsity, 1974), p. 15.
4. Darcy McNickle, *Native American Tribalism* (New York: Oxford U., 1973), p. 78.

I contend that Christianity is a true Indian religion because the Indian assumes his full "Indianness" in Christ, who has provided the way for him to claim his true humanity. Man was created in the image of God (Gen 1:26). By virtue of this fact, he had perfection and eternity; but by his own act of disobedience, he fell—he assumed an abnormal state—and was doomed to die. Thus began the human identity crisis. Because the image of God had been severely scarred by loss of perfection and eternity, the Indian who returns to God through Jesus Christ (John 3:3) is reclaiming the initial state (the normal state) of perfection and eternity. He becomes, at last, a true human being and, therefore, a true Indian.

Udo Middlemann has this to say about identity:

> The Bible . . . traces [man's] identity to an origin beyond the present order of existence. It claims that God—a God who is not confined by immediate existence, who is not a part of what is materially there—has made man in his own image. It claims, therefore, that the primary relationship of man is beyond the immediate physical existence of particulars. . . . [Man's] primary relationship is to God.[5]

Identity—Indianness, in this case—is restored through Jesus Christ, and the primary relationship of man to God is once again operative.

Man cannot liberate himself from the consequences of sin. He is only capable of reformation—a mere rearrangement of parts. God, however, has provided the way to transformation—death of the old followed by birth of the new—through the death of Christ at Calvary. This is true liberation, for it comes from outside man.

Christ addresses sin, which is the root cause of human

---

5. Middlemann, p. 16.

injustice. AIM can offer liberation only (if, indeed, at all) on the social, political, and economic levels. It can bring a change only in physical status. Christ, on the other hand, points out that the social, economic, and political problems of Indians (and all men) are basically a spiritual problem. Man is alienated from God. If man's primary relationship is inoperative, all others will be also.

Christianity, therefore, addresses Indian rights on a very basic level by seeking to correct the human identity crisis, which is a result of alienation. Christianity is the true spiritual movement, for it is involved in the transformation of human character through Christ the Son.

We, as Christians, can press the claims of Christ confidently to Indians, but we must be ready to accept people as they are. If not, we sin against God, for we act contrary to John 3:16. God gave His Son *to* and *for* the world. The world is composed of cultures and nationalities. God, being the Creator of man, can communicate to him in all cultures.

He who is involved in Indian missions and would speak about Christ to Indians should know well the history and value system of the particular Indian people to whom God has sent him to minister. This is the starting point for witness. Let the Holy Spirit be the Guide to effective communication; your witness is a joint venture with Him.

5

Indian Leadership in Indian Evangelism

Billy Graham

For years I have carried both a burden and a guilt concerning the Indian population in the United States. Naturally I have visited many Indian reservations and proclaimed the Gospel there. But during the last couple of years three things have happened that have caused me to be aroused and awakened to the needs of my Indian brothers.

First, the eruption at Wounded Knee. Whatever you may think about it, however you may judge it, however its participants may be criticized, I think they succeeded, at least partially, in bringing Indian grievances to the attention of the American people. Some observers already are predicting that, because the issues and grievances have not been properly dealt with, another confrontation like Wounded Knee might erupt at any time.

The second thing which occurred to arouse me was meeting and talking with Indian leaders such as Tom Claus during our Phoenix Crusade (1974). They showed me something of their evangelical vigor and told me something of their evangelistic needs.

The third thing that aroused me has been reading about the spiritual needs of hundreds of thousands of Indians, many who suffer from poverty, drugs, alcohol, animism, and demonism. All this has caused me to wonder how the Billy Graham Association can participate in helping Native Americans, especially in the fields of social justice and evangelism.

In 1976 the United States celebrated its bicentennial as an independent government. But the ancestry of the Indian cannot be traced to the *Mayflower* or the American Revolution. They were here long before the Europeans arrived. The Indian is the original American.

The Indian has been called "the vanishing American." This is a misnomer. The Indian is the fastest growing ethnic group in America. The Indian population of America today is far greater than when Columbus arrived here from Spain. And those of mixed blood number in the millions.

Today more than thirty thousand Indians are in universities and colleges and technical schools throughout the country. America now has hundreds of fine Indian doctors, engineers, educators, attorneys, and clergymen.

Indians have contributed enormously to the culture and the diet of America, sometimes in rather unexpected ways. For example, Native Americans formed the first temperance organization in the United States. When the government of Pennsylvania refused to regulate the sale of liquor to Indians, the Shawnee tribe held a council in Pittsburgh on March 5, 1737 and voted the prohibition of liquor to themselves.

Many of the early European settlers were concerned for the spiritual life of the Indian. During those earlier years, John Eliot translated the Bible into the language of the Indians of Massachusetts. John Wesley made the long voy-

Indian Leadership in Indian Evangelism 49

age from England to American to preach the Gospel to the Indians of Georgia and other parts of the South. David Brainerd had a soul passion for the Native American. He contracted tuberculosis and died at an early age because he was so desperate to win Indians to Christ. Others, such as Count Zinzendorf and the great New England evangelist, Jonathan Edwards, had a burden and concern for the Indian.

It seems to me it is time once again to emphasize evangelism among all ethnic groups in America, especially among the American Indian. Like other American groups, the Indian today stands at a crossroads, waiting for someone to tell him how to find abundant life. He needs someone to give him a guiding purpose and offer him a goal, someone to make him spiritually whole.

In Romans 13:11 the apostle Paul said, "And that, knowing the time, that now it is high time to awake out of sleep: for now is our salvation nearer than when we believed."

Paul suggests we should know the time. We are living in *changing times*. Minority groups are coming into their own. Gone are the days when the black man, the Spanish-American, or the Indian could be treated as a second-class citizen—without notice!

Evangelicals have a responsibility to try to understand and sympathize with Indian social, cultural, political, and spiritual problems, and especially to help the Indian evangelize his own people. Jesus said, "Ye shall be witnesses unto me both *in Jerusalem* . . . and unto the uttermost parts of the earth" (Acts 1:8, italics added). Indian territory has been part of America's Jerusalem.

Today God is preparing the Indian heart by giving him the Word of God. In 1975 the gospel of John was printed for the first time in the Kobuk Eskimo dialect, and the entire New

Testament was completed for the Papago and Pima people of southern Arizona. The New Testament in Navajo, revised by Navajo Christians themselves, along with Psalms and Proverbs, was publicly dedicated on the Navajo reservation in the spring of 1975. This new edition was almost immediately sold out. Indians will listen more attentively to the Gospel if it is spoken to them in their own native tongue. And tribal languages have not only survived but are on the increase. English is only the "trade" language.

In these changing times, I would urge Indian Christians to come together in a new unity of Evangelicals. I would urge them to make their voices heard among their own people, to present their case to the rest of America. We thank God for the many missionaries who have loved and ministered to Indians through the years, but in these changing times it seems to me that Indians can best be won to Christ by other Indians. The original Americans could turn around and become evangelists to win other Americans to Christ.

Lately several Christian training schools have sprung up, where Indians can receive education for Christian service. Christian leaders are burdened for their people and are seeking ways to win fellow Indians to Christ.

In the past, many missionaries mistakenly tried to convert the Indian to a culture rather than to Christ. They tried to get him to wear white man's suits and give up his traditional dress. They gave him a white shirt and a black tie. They foisted upon him forms of worship strange to his heritage and traditions. Thus, many Indians rebelled against Christianity.

The Native American ought to be approached in a unique way. When he finds Christ, he may want to dress differently, speak his own tribal tongue, and have a long or short service, as he chooses. The Kiowa, the Comanche, and the

Indian Leadership in Indian Evangelism 51

Seminole have composed beautiful Indian hymns by using words of Scripture or testimony put to their own Indian music. If Christ lives in his heart, the Native American is a member of the Body of Christ, and that is what is all-important.

It has been my experience that the Indian is an individualist who can't be pushed around. In order to minister among Indians, one must understand something of the culture, something of the religious background. Yet I have also found that people are the same the world over. Their hearts are the same. The Gospel of Christ is "the power of God unto salvation" (Rom 1:16). If we are faithful in our proclamation of the Gospel, it has its own built-in power to transform and change.

The second thing that I notice in Romans 13:11 is that Paul said, "Now it is high time to awake out of sleep." I am reminded that these are *critical times*.

The Indian communities of America have become infected by too many of the white man's problems, especially drugs and alcohol. Too long have we allowed the forces of Satan to have their way without resistance. We have been too permissive. We have been too compromising. Even many Christians are throwing up their hands and saying it is hopeless. Hopelessness is a powerful force of destruction, not only in minority groups, but in the majority as will.

The late Robert Kennedy said that suicide is higher among Indian young people than any other group in our nation. There is a high suicide rate among young people throughout America. This comes from despair, hopelessness, emptiness, and loneliness.

I can believe this is especially true among Indians, for so many of them have been exploited. In these critical times they are beginning to fight against the injustices and the oppressions of the past. Indians are beginning to fight against disease and illiteracy, but there is still much to do. The Indian is a sleeping giant who is awakening.

True evangelical Christianity is the answer. By nature the Indian is a religious person. Down in the Indian heart, there beats a sense of God. Living close to nature as he does, he knows that the world and the universe are not man-made.

The Indian, like many whites, has been turned off by unconcerned, indifferent Christians. He must be shown that Christ died for him and not just for the white peoples of the world.

Jesus Christ was not a white man. He was not a black or a yellow or a red man. He came from that part of the world that touches Asia, Africa, and Europe. He belongs to the whole human race. It must be demonstrated to the American Indian that the Spirit of Jesus Christ can live in his heart and fulfill the deepest spiritual needs of his life. It can be done. We as Christians are under orders from the Lord Jesus Christ; it must be done!

In our text, the apostle also says, "For now is our salvation nearer." My third suggestion is that these are *challenging times*.

During the Lausanne Congress in 1974 we heard of great spiritual awakenings in Africa, Indonesia, Korea, and in parts of Latin America. For example, the church in Korea is growing four times faster than the population. In Brazil it is growing twice as fast as the population. What is happening among many peoples of the world could happen among the Indians of this country. God is no respecter of persons. He has not bypassed the Indian. The greatest moments of Indian history may lie ahead of us if a great spiritual renewal and awakening should take place.

Someone recently told me that less than a third of the Indian population in America has been evangelized. I was

Indian Leadership in Indian Evangelism

shocked. Certainly our Lord included the Indian when He said, "Other sheep I have, which are not of this fold (John 10:16). Many are tired of the bondage of sin in which they live and would readily respond to the Gospel if they could but hear it.

How wonderful it would be if during the next six months every Christian Indian in America were to win just one other Indian to Christ—then those two were to win four during the next six months—in ten years the whole Indian population of America could be won to Christ. This is not an impossible dream.

I know that there are several Bible schools in North America primarily for Indians. Suppose these converts were sent to Bible schools throughout the country. I can assure you that our organization will help in every way we can to enroll these new converts in Bible schools.

I wish I had an easier, magical word to give. But the commission of Christ applies to Indian Christians as surely as it applies to His first disciples: "Ye shall be witnesses unto me" (Acts 1:8). Just as Peter, James, and John, untutored and untrained, went out to turn their world upside down, Indian believers can witness a turnaround among Indian people through the power of Christ's Gospel.

The head of one Bible school for Indians recently said, "The real answer lies in the trained Indian himself. He has the natural temperament and equipment for the   The truth of this is evidenced in the success of those graduates of the Bible schools who have given themselves to God in behalf of their people."

Send them to Bible training schools, and the Spirit of God will accompany them as they return to communicate the Gospel to their people.

I once spent a Sunday with a Seminole Indian church in

south Florida. The service was held in a modest little chapel of whitewashed cypress boards. The benches were handmade, and the pulpit furnishings were far from elegant. The little chapel was packed with Indians as the Seminole minister stood before his people. A hush came over the audience as he opened the Word of God. With an untutored fluency inspired by the Holy Spirit, he told forth the wondrous message of the love of God in Jesus Christ. This man knew God. His life had been transformed by the power of Christ, and he was sharing his faith in Christ with other Indians. This is the primary way in which Indians will be won to Christ—by other Indians whose hearts have been touched by God.

An Indian girl named Anita was sent to prison for a crime. Awakened by the love of Christ, she wrote the following prayer. I believe it is the heart cry of the thousands of Indian people who long for fellowship with the living God.

> I am lost, I am lonely, I have nowhere to go.
> I am turning to you, Jesus, though I know I have failed you so.
> I have lived a life of evil, drinking, cussing and fighting, too,
> But I beg of you, sweet Jesus, take my hand and see me through.
> My life is filled with sorrow. I am lost to roam and roam.
> I beg of you, sweet Jesus, take my hand and lead me home.
> As I sit here crying in my self-made life of hell,
> I beg of you, sweet Jesus, from my lonely prison cell,
> Take these chains away that bind me, cleanse my soul, Lord, set me free.
> I beg of you, sweet Jesus, hear my cry; I want to serve you until I die.

I beg of you, sweet Jesus, as I reach to take your hand,
Lead me on, blessed Jesus, to your lovely promised land.

6

Christian Education in an Indian Context

Raymond G. Baines

Because of the bad treatment many of our Indian people have received at the hands of the white man for generations, our people, especially some of the older ones, have looked upon formal education as a bad thing. Why? Because the white man brought it.

But education is a tool which we can use to reach the goals that we have set for ourselves in life. Whether we go into business, social services, the medical or legal professions, or into the ministry, education is a tool we can use to fulfill our vocation. But we must always be careful to remember that education is a tool and never an end in itself.

Our primary goal as Christians is to serve Christ in all that we do. I believe that the Holy Spirit helps us as we study and learn. Jesus said something about this in John 14:26 (NASB) when He said, "But the Helper, the Holy Spirit, whom the Father will send in My name, He will teach you all things, and bring to your remembrance all that I said to you."

Too often we limit God by putting Him in a box, so to

speak. We say God works here, especially on Sunday, but doesn't function *out there*—in the so-called secular world. Historians think like this when they talk about *sacred* history and *secular* history. They speak of the Protestant Reformation, the Crusades, John Wesley, John Calvin, and so on, and they call this sacred history. Then they talk about politics, the rise and fall of nations, famine, and war, and they call that secular history. But by faith in the love and power of God, we can affirm that *all* of history is sacred. We can say that history is *His story.* We may not be able to understand or explain all of it, but the omnipotent God is in control, and all will turn out to His glory in the long haul. By faith we proclaim, "All is well."

So I state unequivocally that as we go into education with Christ uppermost in our lives, the Holy Spirit can and will guide us, inspire us, and empower us. What we learn can help us proclaim the Good News of Jesus Christ.

A large part of the national American Indian population is made up of children, youth, and young adults. At an increasing rate year by year, our young people are entering institutions of higher education. At the same time, the majority of Indian pastors have had little formal education in a college or seminary. Many have not finished high school. This means that, increasingly, a communication gap is developing between the traditional Indian ministry and our young people who are going on to higher education. Education is one of the important tools by which we can bridge this gap.

By all of this I do not mean in any way to belittle the traditional ministry of Indian pastors. For many generations they have been on the firing line for Jesus Christ. They are committed and dedicated Christians who, out of a limited educational background, have served faithfully and honorably in Indian country across the nation. They have at times

Christian Education in an Indian Context

served in very difficult situations at a salary level far below that of our white brothers with college and seminary training.

I am throwing out this challenge to you because I want our Christian ministry to *our own people* to be the best ministry possible for the good of our people and for the glory of Christ. If we are going to keep our young people in the church and challenge them to enter church-related vocations, then we must challenge them on a level that they can understand and appreciate. Education is one of the tools by which we can do this.

What should education accomplish for our people? Primarily I would say that education should help develop discipline within our people. The Greek word translated *disciple* is the same root word from which we get *discipline*. A disciple is more than merely a follower; he is a student, a scholar, one who gets better and stronger through learning. The account in Luke 10:38-42 is an illustration of two types of followers of Jesus of Nazareth, and they are with us even today. Martha was caught up with busy work. Mary chose the better part. And in sitting at the Master's feet and learning, Mary was a prime example of what a disciple really is. *Discipline* is defined as "training that develops self-control and efficiency."

Consider for a moment the various professions, whether the legal, medical, business, or industrial professions or the ministry. You will note that those who reach the uppermost ranks of their profession are those who have discipline and exercise it.

One Indian pastor, himself a leader of pastors, told me that there were ministers under his charge who studied only when they felt moved and only made pastoral calls when it was convenient. These men spent much of their time fishing, camping, hunting, or working on their automobiles. This reminds me of Peter after he had denied his Lord, and Jesus had been crucified. Even after Jesus Christ had revealed Himself to the disciples, an evident doubt remained in their hearts. Out of this doubt, Peter pitifully exclaimed, "I am going fishing." He influenced others, who also said, "We will also come with you" (John 21:3, NASB). Jesus had called the apostles to follow Him. He called them from their fishing boats and nets and from other means of livelihood to a life of dedicated service, a life of obedience and discipline. Today He has called us to do our utmost in order to attain His highest—to be disciplined and diligent for the glory and honor of our Christ. He has called us to be students and learners—to live a life of discipline and diligence.

Through the discipline of formal education we can come to know ourselves—and our people—better. Out of my own experience, through the study of philosophy, psychology, sociology, and history, I have come to know myself much better. And in understanding myself better, I have come to know others better. The purpose of education for those of us who are followers of Christ is to gain tools by which we can serve Him to the greatest possible degree. For us as Christians, the core of education is Christ.

It has always concerned our tribal leaders to see our young people leave home to acquire an education and then never return to give leadership to their own people. This is a valid concern, especially as it relates to the Christian Church. But the picture is even more bleak. I quote here from an article entitled "Leadership Crisis in the Indian Church," which appeared recently in the bimonthly *Yakima Drum Beat*, published by the Disciples of Christ Mission to the Yakima Indians in the State of Washington:

Christian Education in an Indian Context

A recent survey of Indian church leadership revealed that the Indian church in *seven denominations* will virtually be without ordained Indian clergy within a decade unless the present methods of church career development are changed, and soon. The "typical" Indian pastor works in a denomination which now has fewer ordained Indian clergy than in 1949, despite the millions of dollars and publicity about self-development in recent years.

Present age of the typical pastor is 52 years and the median age of the Indian population is 20 years. The typical Indian pastor is at least 32 years older than most of his parishioners and approximately 10 years older than non-Indian pastors serving Indian congregations.

Within the next ten years, approximately fifty percent of the Indian pastors will retire. Despite the youthfulness of the Indian population, the typical pastor does not have an active youth program.

Today the statistically typical pastor entered his church career at age 35, at least 10 years later than non-Indian pastors. He is bilingual in his ministry, has not attended a theological seminary, but has attended a workshop in the past year. In 1973-74 there were only three Indian students in Protestant seminaries included in this study.

There is a crisis in leadership within the American Indian church. Our Indian young people need to follow the leading of Christ into the ministry. Most of the denominations with which I have worked in the field of Indian ministries are acutely aware of this need, but none of them is doing much about it by way of a dynamic program of recruitment and education.

It is not only a question of young people entering seminary; they must enter a good *evangelical* seminary. There are many good, academically responsible seminaries. But let me suggest the possibility of an American Indian seminary and possibly even a college. It may be that a graduate school program for the ministry could be developed in conjunction with Bacone College. Or a Department of Indian Ministries might be developed at a good, accredited, evangelical college or university which would also include an Indian seminary—planned, implemented, and operated by Indian staff.

The "classroom without walls" concept, which is becoming increasingly utilized, could be valuable here. This educational method sends the faculty out to the students, who are given a concentrated course for a couple of weeks or over several weekends. Undergraduate and graduate college credit is given. This makes it possible for the student who otherwise might be kept from finishing his training in the ministry to study in his community while he is employed. I assume that there are other methods of education for the ministry that we could look at.

In conclusion, let me reiterate that education is important, very important. If we are to keep our young people, not only as church members but also as church leaders, we must provide a high level of challenge and the opportunity for responsible academic training. This is especially true as an increasing number of our young people are going on to higher education.

While a good, academically sound education will provide many dynamic tools with which to work in our ministry, education is never an end in itself. The purpose of a responsible program of education for the ministry is to provide us tools through which we can win our people to Christ and bring glory to Him. The core is Christ, and the message is His Good News.

7

Working with the Indian Church

Thomas Francis, Charlie Lee, Jerry Sloan

The Great Commission establishes the universality of the Gospel. The Gospel has the ability to take root and prosper in any community, regardless of geographical or cultural boundaries.

The Christian witness has gone forth to Indian peoples in North America for four centuries. Many Indians have responded. Born-again Indian believers, empowered by the Holy Spirit, have demonstrated that they can carry out the Great Commission as well as any other missionary. The message appeals to all, so it has met the spiritual needs of Indians.

In spite of this, there is a marked absence of indigenous Indian churches. Many Indian communities are still highly resistant to the Gospel message. There is a lack of missionary vision. Why?

One reason is missionary paternalism. This speaks of methods and approaches perpetuated by sponsoring mission organizations and missionaries. In some instances, the missionary has become an undisputed master; the people are treated like irresponsible children. This has produced an overprotective, bureaucratic mission, which is unwilling to give up control and to delegate responsibilities to the converts.

Another reason we find relatively few ongoing indigenous churches is the lack of understanding, not only of Indians by missionaries, but also of the nature of the church by Indians.

Though there may be no visible natural or geographical boundaries, in many ways the Indian culture is just as foreign to the white man as are the cultures of the Mexican, African, or Asian. The Indian's language, customs, and religious beliefs are just as real to him as these things are to those peoples in the "regions beyond." Unfortunately, many missionaries have failed to take that fact into consideration, and the lack of understanding on the part of the church in America has been even greater.

The Indian, in turn, has little or no concept of the local church, principally due to lack of teaching. However, he does have a concept of what a mission is, what missionaries are, and what they are for. A mission is a place where you go to receive. It is similar to a welfare agency, except it has religious services. The missionaries are employed by the mission to dispense charity to Indians. At special times (Christmas, Easter) they receive an abundance of things to distribute. Some even have a place where you can stay overnight. They have vehicles to carry you to places you need to go, such as hospitals or clinics. Indians don't know how or where the missionaries get funds for all these blessings. They seem to know a source that is limitless, because some build schools, hospitals, and missions.

Similarities in methods of operation and government between the mission and the Bureau of Indian Affairs make it

Working with the Indian Church

difficult for the Indian to differentiate between the two, except that one of them does not have religious services.

Too often the Indian has been willing to accept the role of an object of charity that the missionary designates for him. His passive role is that of a dependent recipient. Evangelism is the missionary's job—he gets paid for it.

To carry out evangelism and to build an indigenous church in the light of these misunderstandings are not easy tasks, but they can be done!

The times are changing, and the attitudes of the Indian people are changing also. There is a growing cultural and ethnic identity that approaches a nationalistic attitude on the part of some of them. It could very well be that the door to many areas under the control of the Indian will soon be closed to the white missionary. In such a situation, the full weight of responsibility will be on the Indian church.

As Indians, we will always be accepted by our Indian brothers because we are Indians, but they will not always accept our message. They have good reason to be suspicious of our intentions, but we can't give up on the first try when presenting the Gospel.

The methods of evangelism must vary according to the need of each particular village, reservation, or urban situation. We must, first of all, know the type of people we are dealing with, their cultural background, and their religious background. Of necessity our work must be done on the grass-roots level, taking an interest in their everyday life, living a Christian testimony before them, becoming involved in their sports, and building a bond of confidence in an informal atmosphere in order that we can begin to share our understanding of the Gospel of Jesus Christ.

There are people who in the past have refused to embrace the white man's religion. They have kept their own form of worship, and the spirit world is very real to them. The opposition of the powers of darkness can be very real, and the Word falls on deaf ears.

Where there is no conflict with truth, the Gospel is adaptable to native culture and psychology. God blesses even in a primitive hogan service where the Indians sometimes chant the hymns rather than sing, American style. A minister of the Gospel must approach such situations equipped with the whole armor of God and fully aware of the power of the Holy Spirit to work in every situation.

The field of Indian missions is not one for fly-by-night evangelism in which the evangelistic team is in and out the same night and never seen again. Especially for our Indian people, this is a fantasy. The Great Commission involves teaching and making disciples. To do this requires dedicated labor over a period of time, with the formation of indigenous churches wherever there are bodies of believers.

To build a church that is self-supporting, self-governing, and self-propagating, the pastor (not a missionary) must have a clear concept of his plan of action. His assignment is to build a church, not to set up a mission. The words *mission* and *missionary* are taboo because of the connotation they have in the mind of the Indian. The pastor must keep a proper perspective on his relationship to his converts.

He must realize and understand that his ministry as a church builder is transitory; he is not indispensable. He must train his converts to become responsible and productive. The church must not become dependent on him, but rather, he must depend on the church.

The pastor must keep his eyes open for potential teachers and leaders, and it becomes his responsibility to train them. His ability to build competence in these people

Working with the Indian Church

and to train them properly will be proven by the responsibility his people accept.

If we have faith to pray for and receive material help, why can't we have faith to expect God to raise up teachers and leaders? The pastor must ask God to give him capable people—you get what you aim for. Whenever a responsibility can be filled by a local convert, the pastor should expect to train him for the position rather than recruit someone from outside the congregation.

To build a self-supporting church, the pastor must begin to teach the converts a systematic plan of giving. The Bible has directives for that. He must have faith to trust God to give his people jobs and income to support the church and its pastor. From the very beginning he should work on phasing out any outside subsidy as local support builds. Overfunding from the outside develops dependency and kills initiative. It tends to dull any sense of responsibility, robs people of a blessing, and weakens the spiritual and moral fiber of the church.

The pastor must involve his people in handling the funds and developing a good budget. He should let them keep the books and pay the bills. Secrecy on money matters breeds doubt and suspicion.

To build a self-propagating church, the pastor must assign teaching responsibility to the converts. He must pray for them, select them, teach them, train them, and assign them leadership responsibility.

Even on our Indian reservations there are many young people who have gained much knowledge of the business world outside the reservation. Much of what they have learned there can be rechanneled into spiritual use. Thus, we can find many young "Timothys." We have a shortage of capable, young preachers only because we have not encouraged them to take leadership roles within the congregation.

We talk about the world getting smaller because of our technological advance. Let us take advantage of this technology for the cause of Christ. Radio and television are being used to share the Gospel of our Lord Jesus Christ. Tape recorders and cassettes are being used extensively in very practical ways to edify Christians and to build Christian Indian leadership.

Think for a moment about the apostle Paul. If he had the equipment, knowledge, and mobility we have today, how would he take advantage of these means for the glory of God in the propagation of the Gospel? Would he not train Christian Indian leaders, build indigenous churches, have a national Christian Indian association? Our increased mobility can help bring about a pastoral leadership exchange across the country or across many miles of an Indian reservation.

Learning from other churches within a single tribe or across tribal boundaries helps a Christian leader gain new insights and renews his vision for his church and area of service. It releases creative ideas. His ministry takes on a new and deeper meaning, and it gains a challenge; at the same time, some of the prejudices and stereotyped ideas are removed. Through interaction with other leaders, new evangelism techniques can be explored and leadership training ideas exchanged.

We desire to see among our people indigenous churches that share the life of the community in which they are planted and find within themselves the ability to govern, support, and reproduce themselves. We desire to see the Great Commission carried out among our own people by

Working with the Indian Church

our own people. We need each other in this work, and each of us has a job to do.

God says in 2 Chronicles 7:14, "If my people, which are called by my name, shall humble themselves, and pray, and seek my face, and turn from their wicked ways; then will I hear from heaven, and will forgive their sin, and will heal their land." This is God's promise for us and our people.

8

Developing Lay Leadership

Claudio B. Iglesias

Historically, the idea of a leader is not a new concept to Indians, whether here in the United States, in Central America, or in South America. Indian people have always chosen their own leaders, usually to serve for a lifetime. Among the tribes, one becomes a leader by different means, but the important factor is that the man chosen to lead comes from the people and has proven himself. More important, he is a man the people can trust.

With this in mind, why are we finding it so hard to develop Christian lay leaders among Indian peoples today? White missionaries have worked among Indian tribes for many years. Some denominations have labored seventy years or more without a sign of a strong lay leadership.

I believe that in some Indian tribes a white missionary represents a "threat" to their own leader, a threat caused by a communication gap. This is especially true when a tribal language is universally used among the people. Usually the missionary cannot speak the language of the people. Just when he begins to enjoy the trust and confidence of the people and begins to communicate with them, he leaves, and another missionary begins all over again trying to bridge the gap. There is very little continuity. I presume this is why some are saying that missionaries have failed the Indians.

Some tribes have developed a strong lay witness, however. Among them are the Tzeltal of southern Mexico; their neighbors, the Chol; and the San Blas Kuna people of Panama. Since much of my experience has been among my own people, the Kunas, let me share with you some ideas that seemed to work, under the guidance of the Holy Spirit, in Panama.

My brother Lonnie—Dr. A. L. Iglesias—is now with the Lord. But the work he began, and in which we shared for fifteen years, continues to grow through dedicated San Blas believers.

The majority of these are laymen, such as the four who are responsible for the thriving mission in the city of Panama. During their summer vacation, young people of this mission plan and carry out evangelistic meetings in villages out in the islands from which they originally came. This fresh witness is making an impact on villages which have been exposed to some form of Christianity for several generations. A young Kuna medical doctor in one of these island villages has become a witnessing lay leader. The same mission group which sponsors the island campaigns has sent two lay leaders to begin a new work among the jungle Kunas in an untouched section of the country.

How is such leadership developed?

Above all, I believe that the lay leader must have a sense of call to his own people. The pastor or missionary must be sensitive to this. The Reverend James W. Nelson, writing on "Obstacles to Church Growth," states, "It is difficult to con-

Developing Lay Leadership

vince some people that the Holy Spirit has power to take any person and use him effectively. It is hard for a well-educated missionary to accept the fact that an unlearned layman may do a better job of sharing his faith with his fellows than the missionary." Sometimes a well-educated Indian missionary or pastor has the same problem. We blame white missionaries sometimes for paternalism. We who are Indian must be careful that we do not show the same paternalistic attitude.

I cannot emphasize strongly enough that the approach to lay leadership must be within the context of the culture. The tribal worker should not try to force it into a foreign mold. He must understand tribal norms and values and be aware of ethical and moral attitudes, theological concepts, and practices regarding the individual and the family. He must know what are considered social and civic responsibilities concerning possessions.

Such a broad understanding is difficult without a knowledge of the language. A speaking knowledge of the language used by the people is basic to an effective ministry and a relationship of mutual trust. Even though I am a native Kuna, I had to "relearn" my language, when I returned home following my education, before my people showed confidence in me as a leader.

Today among the San Blas Kuna of Panama there is a growing lay leadership based upon some forty years of Christian witness. My late brother felt, and I also feel, that any lasting change in a life must come from within, and that preaching *at* people is not the answer.

Teaching children in our mission elementary schools was one avenue for change, since no public schools existed on many islands. Another important avenue for witness was the evening town meetings in the congress hall, where community affairs are discussed and the traditions of the tribe are chanted by town leaders. We found a ready audience for Bible teaching there, just as Jesus did in the synagogue of His day.

One of the needs we soon sensed, however, was for the Word of God to be translated into our language. A Bible in English or Spanish was not enough. God had to speak Kuna. The translation of the gospel of Mark was begun by my brother and a group of other native speakers. Now the New Testament translation, completed by native speakers and published by the American Bible Society, is being used in services and read in thatched huts.

It is important to develop and equip lay leaders at their own level. Many of our young men had not gone beyond the sixth grade, and most of the older ones had never attended school at all. Since they depended upon their memories, we went slowly and repeated often. Teaching first the "milk of the Word," we chose to give a general view of the Bible and then focused upon the life of Jesus Christ, how to become a Christian, and how to grow in faith. We found that certain parables and events of the Bible are more readily understood than others by our people because of similarities to the culture of San Blas, which involves boats and fishing as well as farming.

We would travel by boat from mission points to other island villages or along the coast. Always several young men would go with us to visit. As they grew in their Christian experience, they would be ready to share their testimonies, lead in hymn singing, and take turns at teaching the Bible lesson we had previously prepared together. Sunday schools were established in neighboring communities and taught by these young believers, with an older believer to help with the town leaders.

Developing Lay Leadership

One reason these boys liked to go along was that on the trips we would often take time for fun and fellowship. These young men were good fishermen and we wanted them also to be good "fishers of men," so we shared the work and the visiting, and watched for good witnessing opportunities. Even though the culture demands that more mature men have the strongest voice in the community, these young men were permitted to be heard, especially when they had Bible stories to tell.

In San Blas, like anywhere else, growth in the Christian life is not without struggle against temptation. With the help of the Holy Spirit, we tried to teach our young believers the spirit of love. We prayed with our boys and we prayed for them. We wanted them to have a consistent Christian life, a life that pointed to the Saviour. He had to become the center of their lives.

As a missionary, I could have some freedom from the demands of the tightly knit community life, such as the ritual drinking feasts. But these young men had to meet all that was expected of them. I tried to be available to my boys at all times, and especially when certain pressures were being put on them to act in a way contrary to Christian principles.

As years passed, many Kunas began moving to the cities of Panama, where more jobs are available and there is opportunity to further their education. Whole families are now moving to the cities.

It isn't easy to adapt to a new situation, especially in a foreign culture. Yet I have been thrilled to visit Kuna missions in Colon and Panama City—missions led by young laymen who had come to Christ out in the islands. Of these leaders, some are still students. One has become a professor at a university, but he is busy every weekend in preaching and witnessing. Pianists, Sunday school teachers, and preachers are all native Kuna with some training and a zeal in their hearts to share Christ. Members of the mission rent the building and maintain a daily witness in the noisy, crowded area of the inner city.

Each vacation they plan a crusade to one of the islands "back home." They have held revival services on the very island where my brother and I were born and where we were once told we could not live as missionaries or preach the Gospel. I'm told that many found Christ as Saviour.

What we learned and experienced in developing lay leadership in Panama may not be applicable in the United States. But even here the message should not be oriented to the society from which the pastor or missionary has come. It should be a message of Christian concern for the Indian where he is in this world of complicated social change. If lay leaders are to be encouraged and trained, there should be a more positive emphasis on Christian ethics based upon love.

The Gospel is meant to be shared by every believer, not just the clergy. A lay leader becomes an effective witness only when he is willing to let the Holy Spirit mold his life. Potential Christian leaders are right there, among our neighbors; let us do our best to find them, to encourage them, and to trust them.

9

The Wonder World of Words

Raymond L. Gowan

Throughout the long history of Indian missions (almost three hundred years), Christian literature geared to Indian thought and culture, in either English or the numerous tribal languages, has been almost nonexistent.

The Bible has been translated into some Indian languages, the very first one in America being John Eliot's Indian Bible, published in the language of an Algonquin tribe located in what is now Massachusetts. Today there is no surviving remnant of the tribe. Pastor John Eliot and Job Neustan, an Indian whom Eliot had rescued from a slave-driving farmer, labored for years on the translation. Eliot himself paid for the first fifteen hundred Bibles. As a result of Eliot's great personal interest and missionary activity, many Indians became Christians.

James Evans, an Englishman, translated the Word of God into Cree for Canadian Indians. His work has had a lasting impact in vast areas of Canada. Many other translations for the Indians have been completed, including recent ones by the Wycliffe Bible Translators. But the impact and effectiveness of such translations are limited to the tribe speaking the specific language of that version.

Although in some areas the Gospel is still presented in the languages of the tribes, the standard of communication for most of these groups in the United States and Canada is fast becoming English. In the past twenty-five years, literacy has made great strides among Native Americans.

In 1962 I made a survey in British Columbia and found some of the Indian areas had only begun elementary education in 1957. Only a few years ago here in the States, a mere handful of Indian students were graduating from high school. Now thousands are receiving their diplomas and going on to college. The University of New Mexico has seven hundred of these students, and this is being duplicated elsewhere.

As Indians and other Native Americans become more literate and more knowledgeable through formal education, radio, and television, an immense hunger for Indian-related literature develops. This no doubt accounts for the many new Indian periodicals that have appeared in recent years. New ones continue to cross my desk every few weeks. But precious few of them have much spiritual or positive content.

Benjamin Franklin once said, "Give me 26 lead soldiers and I will conquer the world." Long ago the Communists and the promoters of false cults discovered those twenty-six lead soldiers—the alphabet. They understood the value of attractive literature placed in the right hands. Even today, while their printing presses hum, Christian people seem content to sleep on, with only a few awake to the gigantic possibilities in Christian literature as a powerful tool in evangelism.

In 1967 I purchased the biggest printing press my faith

The Wonder World of Words

would allow. I personally coaxed eight thousand copies of *Indian Life* off that little press in August of that year. It was a tiny sheet, almost colorless. But it was an instant success. Why? The hour had come! Indians could easily relate and identify with the Indian news, stories, prayers, and recipes, and the testimonies of Indians who have something to say.

In 1974, Native Americans devoured more than 650,000 copies of *Indian Life*. It is now an eight-page color tabloid newspaper, four times larger than the first issue. Instead of being issued twice a year, it has become a bimonthly with a current circulation of 100,000 copies.

This points up the tremendous hunger out there, right now, for Christian literature that is informative, positive, uplifting, and believable.

Previous to publishing *Indian Life*, I don't remember ever receiving a letter from an Indian in my eighteen years of labor among them. But don't let anyone tell you Indians can't or don't write letters. Since the advent of *Indian Life*, communications by the thousands have poured into my office from Indians all the way from Mexico to the Arctic. And I can count on one hand the letters opposing such Christian literature.

Listen to what they say: "It is pleasant to my taste!" "It is beautiful." "I am fascinated and intrigued!" "I am on a waiting list to read *Indian Life*. By the time it gets to me it is worn out. Please send a copy of my own!" "Keep up the good work!"

Chairman Mao Tse-Tung believed every citizen of China should read his philosophy. So he published a book, *The Quotations of Chairman Mao*. Norman Vincent Peale heard about this and decided a book should be published for every human being, giving the quotations of Jesus Christ. I liked his idea and decided every Indian should have the sayings of Jesus in words easy to understand. So I had one hundred thousand booklets published with the title, *Words of Life from Jesus Christ*. This, too, was an instant success. The Scripture text was taken from the most lucid, limited-vocabulary English version of the New Testament, *The New Life Testament*, prepared by Gleason Ledyard for Indians and Eskimo.

Only after a person has been in this field for a time does he realize today's tremendous need and wonderful opportunities. Much more sound, sensible Christian literature is needed for our Native Americans. I am told that many Indians read grocery fliers over and over, even though they have no intention of buying anything. They have the time and desire to read! They will take reading material away from you, devour it in one sitting, then turn and ask for more.

Years ago a minister friend of mine handed out a few tracts near Wounded Knee. Seventeen years later he happened to be in the same community. An old Sioux approached my friend, saying, "Oh, I know you." Off came his big black hat. Reaching inside the hatband, he pulled out some well-worn tracts, proudly remarking, "You gave me these."

Never have our Indian people heard so many voices! Confusion often reigns among many who do not know our Lord. An old Indian once told me, "You are too late! Twenty-five years too late!" Pointing to an old Indian, he continued, "What can you do for him? What can you do for me?" Singling out an Indian youth nearby, he continued, "*They* won't even listen to you now!"

God forgive us for taking so long to wake up. Though we are late, we are **not too late for multi**plied thousands, even

The Wonder World of Words

millions if we count the Indians in Mexico, Central America, and South America.

Through my long contact with Indians, I have become aware of a great spiritual hunger among the Indians of North America. A young lad wrote the other day, "I have never read the Bible. Please send me one." An Apache girl's letter was filled with mountains of trouble. She said, "I write to you because you have love and understanding. I have never had this before." The psychology of the printed word—"It is in print; it must therefore be true"—is certainly having its impact through the pages of *Indian Life*.

This wonder world of words, slanted to the Indian people, is an arena of staggering opportunity. Printed words, seasoned with prayer and freighted with the power of the Holy Spirit, have become holy incendiaries lighting tiny fires all across Indian country. I firmly believe that Christian literature, if continued and increased, will bring about the greatest spiritual awakening ever known among the native people of North America!

The field is being covered with Christian literature in a way not possible by any other method. Multiplied thousands who never attend church are being evangelized in the quietness and privacy of their own homes. Many priests and nuns are placing large orders for Testaments and literature for the Indians. A Catholic priest has approached his archbishop to present the merits of our Christian literature for circulation in Catholic missions.

The hour has come for a massive thrust of Christian literature oriented to the Indian people—produced, sponsored, and edited by leading Christian Indians. The potential is unlimited! It will be an instant success!

The field is still white unto harvest! Let us stand together in making the very best of the staggering opportunities before us today in literature evangelism. Together we shall continue to light the fires of a great spiritual awakening among Native Americans everywhere!

10

Language Problems Facing Native Americans

Randall H. Speirs

Christian leadership must be founded on a person's call from God, the recognition of this call by fellow Christians (the Church), and preparation for the job to be done. This preparation must include a thorough knowledge of God's Word, as well as other subject matter, to fit a person for the specific leadership task to which God calls him. A teacher of preschool Sunday school children, a preacher or evangelist, and a superintendent of an association of churches will each need different types of total preparation for their work beyond a knowledge of the Scriptures, and even in their knowledge of the Scriptures. The ability or opportunity to acquire the necessary knowledge and skills will depend to a large extent on one's language background.

Among Native America people today, there is a wide variation of facility in English, and therefore a vast difference in general educational background. Some come from homes and communities in which only English is spoken; they know nothing of their own tribal tongue. This home background does not guarantee, however, that their language abilities and general education have prepared them for desired careers. For example, their education may have been in substandard schools. I have heard that many graduates of schools operated by the Bureau of Indian Affairs (BIA) find it difficult to compete with graduates from public schools, although I have no concrete evidence on this. Non-BIA schools in reservation areas might just as easily be below the national standard.

Further, the Native American's acquisition of English may have been in communities where substandard or nonstandard English is spoken. Nonstandard English may be the only language spoken there, as is the case in some black communities today. Of course, if the individual's activity is to be confined to his home community, he will not experience the handicap in communication that he would if he tried to function elsewhere. Nonetheless, he could still be hampered by his inability to effectively use study guides written in standard English.

On the other hand, speaking only English could be a handicap if other segments of the tribe are actively using the native tongue. Then the individual's ministry will be limited to communicating with them in English, since English is his only language.

Those who are bilingual—in their tribal language and in English—could also face problems. A true bilingual is someone who is able to speak on and understand with facility any topic in both languages. Such persons are very rare. More typical is a person who may understand better than he can speak in one language or the other. Or a bilingual person may get along well in one or the other language in certain conversation areas, but not so well in others. In religious matters, for example, his schooling in the Bible may have been totally in English. His understand-

Language Problems Facing Native Americans

ing of some Bible words may be totally in English. He may have some grasp of words like *justification* and *sanctification* but be quite unable to express them in his second language. This will be a severe problem for him if he is to minister to his own people in the native language. On the other hand, if he is to minister to English-speaking people, he may have a problem with the language in which he thinks. Very often a bilingual person is not speaking English as much as he is translating thought patterns from his own language into English. This can limit his ability to communicate effectively, even if his use of the English vocabulary is completely correct.

Some solutions for the above problems are suggested:

1. Some training in communication may be needed. One who does have a good background in English should discipline himself to use English at a level that communicates well to the people to whom he ministers. Thus, he will neither "show off" his linguistic ability nor "talk down" to the people. One does not need big words and complicated sentences to explain profound thoughts (the writings of C. S. Lewis are a good example of this kind of communication).
2. No Native American should be ashamed of his lack of ability in English. The proper kind of pride—not the kind that the Bible speaks against, which makes a person try to put himself above others—will cause a person to say, "I am supremely important in the sight of God, because He sent His Son to die for me. I will use what I have to the glory of God."

The remedy is to admit freely one's need and then seek help. Perhaps remedial English courses can be taken. Perhaps simplified materials can be used, understanding that the word *simplified* does not mean cutting down on meaningful content, but using simpler words to convey the same thoughts. In some cases, simplified Sunday school material has been rejected by those who needed such material, just because they did not want to admit their need of a simpler language level.

Native American Christian leaders should be urged to use some of the modern English versions. It should be remembered that spiritual barriers already stand in the way, keeping people from the Gospel. There is no sense in putting up language barriers, too, by using a form of English that even many well-educated Anglos have a hard time understanding. Here, perhaps, a knowledge of the history of the English Bible would help those persons who are bound to older, though not well-understood, translations.

3. A Native American Christian leader who can minister to his own people in the tribal tongue should not hesitate to do so. This should go without saying, and perhaps it is not much of a problem in the United States. But in Mexico, for example, some Indian preachers use Spanish even though they can barely get along in it. They do this despite the fact that a large part of their congregation, particularly the women, understand nothing of what they say. This strange behavior is brought about by the wrong kind of pride. Spanish is the language of prestige, and the preacher wants everyone to appreciate his ability to speak it.

Certainly we must be realistic and recognize that everyone in the United States these days needs to know English to get along in our economy. But communicating the great truths of Almighty God is far more important than the "almighty dollar." Give Caesar what is his, and give God what is His. Any formal training institution

(such as a Bible school) should not only emphasize the use of the tribal tongue but should give practical courses in how to communicate the Gospel in that native language. Instruction should particularly emphasize ways of expressing theological terms (such as *justification* and *sanctification* mentioned above, plus a long list of others) in clearly understood phraseology of the native languages.
4. Finally, a translation of the Word of God should be provided for any tribe in which the language is still used in daily life. One Indian man in Guatemala asked the founder of the Wycliffe Bible Translators, "If your God is so smart, how come He doesn't speak my language?" The Bible is God's Book, not the English or Spanish or German or French people's book, and it should be available to all people in the God-given tongue that is most meaningful to them, either intellectually or psychologically. The great surge in bilingual education will produce readers of native tongues who will be reading whatever is available for them to read. Why not God's Word, too?

If the Scriptures are already available in his language, the Native American should expect to become a fluent reader so this valuable tool can be used to reach the lost for Christ.

11

Obstacles to Economic Development

Kogee Thomas

Indian economic development problems are causing growing national concern. The rising mood of Indian assertiveness, combined with a heightening national awareness, has elevated the "first American" in our collective consciousness. The legacy of injustice imposed on the American Indian by the white man is made even worse by the inability to provide effective redress.

The individual Indian is often torn between a desire to remain with his diminishing land to recover the essence of his culture, and a temptation to adapt to the nonreservation world so that he may increase his material well-being. In either case, he is often deprived of a genuine opportunity to be successful.

Because Indians have been unable to sell, transfer, or consolidate their inherited rights to allotted lands, except in a very few tribes, these properties have been frozen in an unusable state. The only benefit possible is through rental. Since leasers are usually white men, the limited land base for an Indian economy is further decreased by this leasing system.

The allotment system established by the federal government to provide homesteads on which Indian families might become self-sufficient farmers has been in itself defeating. First, many Indians had no technological background or knowledge of the economic system on which American family agriculture is based. Second, Indians who were nonagricultural in prereservation times felt no motivation to take up farming. Their economic problem on the reservation has been developing over a long period of time.

Economic development under the overall control of tribal governments is one way in which Indians can both affect their current situation and build for a more self-sufficient future. Cooperative setting of priorities and planning by indigenous Indian leadership can provide the necessary element for community involvement in the development process. And genuine economic development, consisting of thoughtful identification of exploitable reservation resources, capable development of enterprises based on these assets, and the use of initial revenues and profits to fuel subsequent growth can provide strong support for the evolution of a more prosperous, self-reliant Indian people.

Let us look for a moment at what the late Senator Robert F. Kennedy called "the cold statistics which illuminate a national tragedy and a national disgrace."

Most Indian families live in varying degrees of poverty. The basic causes are cultural differences from the non-Indian society, the lack of educational opportunities, and underdevelopment of reservation-based resources. These handicaps are aggravated by geographical isolation from the rest of society and a set of values that has been characterized as "an intense attachment to native soil, a reverent

Obstacles to Economic Development

disposition toward habitat and ancestral ways, and a restraint on individual self-seeking in favor of family and community."[1]

The federal government holds title in trust for Indians to approximately forty million acres of tribally owned land and eleven million acres of individually owned land. Possession of land gives Indians a sense of contribution. This psychological fact, which has its counterpart in some non-Indian depressed areas, helps explain why Indians often choose to remain on land that currently offers limited economic support.

The average Indian income is 70 percent below the national average; his unemployment rate normally hovers around ten times the national average. The average American Indian's life expectancy is seven years less than the national average.

These statistics are neither new nor surprising. Today's Indians, however, have seen the material riches of the outside world. Painfully aware of their poverty, they are angered and impatient. This has created an explosive situation. Many are saying that "if something isn't done, the young Indians may turn to violence."

The social and economic conditions of many Indian people, when compared to that of the general population, almost defy comprehension. Adult Indians living on reservations are, as a group, only half as well educated as other citizens; their average annual income is two-thirds less. Nine out of ten of their homes are comparatively unfit for human habitation.

Until 1961 little effort was made to alleviate the Indian's housing problems. Even today the total of all federal pro-

---

1. Special Senate Subcommittee on Indian Education, "Indian Education—A National Tragedy—A National Challenge." (Washington, D.C.: U.S. Government Printing Office, 1969), p. ix.

grams directed toward improving Indian housing does not keep pace with continuing deterioration and dilapidation. The conditions under which they live—particularly the lack of safe, available water and adequate waste-disposal facilities—are in large part responsible for the high incidence of preventable diseases among Indian populations. The most common infectious diseases among Indians are gastroenteritis and streptococcal infections. Trachoma, which has virtually disappeared among this country's general population, still affects many Indians. Whereas the average life expectancy for the nation's population as a whole is 70.2 years, that for an Indian is only 63.8 years.

Upgrading the economy on Indian reservations will be a long, difficult, complicated process. To make the kind of impact that would truly alleviate the despair permeating most Indian reservations, an economic development program must be massive and must reach a majority of families simultaneously.

Programs to increase Indian employment in agriculture and to bring industry to Indian reservations have been in existence for years, with only limited success. Few industrial establishments have been sufficiently venturesome to move to Indian country. Fewer still have remained for any appreciable length of time.

In agriculture, the amount of money required to create and sustain a viable economic enterprise for a single family is so great that the limited funds available have permitted only a handful of Indians to establish such enterprises. As a result, in almost every situation Indians sit by idle and unemployed while non-Indian businessmen, farm operators, and ranchers reap the profits from the utilization of Indian resources, land, and business.

Industrial development has often been regarded as the

Obstacles to Economic Development

most favorable long-run solution to the economic problems of Indians preferring to remain on reservations. But during the last few years the conception of both economists and policy-makers regarding the role of agriculture in economic development has undergone an important evolution. Where once agriculture was viewed as a passive partner in the development process, it is now more often regarded as an active coequal partner with the industrial sector.

We have learned that agricultural improvement constitutes only a part of the general economic development within a nation. Leaders in many less-developed countries have mistakenly ignored agriculture, concentrating wholly on industrial development. But neither is the answer to swing all the way over to agriculture, ignoring industry. A modern economy can advance only through simultaneous progress in both agriculture and industry. The exact nature and dimensions of the advance in each sector must be adapted to the country's resources, markets, and other economic characteristics.

It would seem that this same approach to economic development—that is, agriculture and industry advancing simultaneously—would hold true with respect to Indian economic development. However, agriculture, in most instances, can support only a minor part of the population of any reservation. Other types of development must be depended on, such as public works programs, industrial development, and business and commercial ventures occurring simultaneously with agricultural development. When we look at the process of economic development in this light, we soon realize the tremendous task that lies ahead for Indian people with respect to solving their social and economic problems. The combined efforts of tribal, government, and private programs toward selective industrialization and business development could transform the economic situation on many reservations.

The industrial development of Indian reservations is a comparatively recent phenomenon. Prior to 1960, only four factories were located on Indian reservations. The recent expansion in business activity, plus the efforts of the Area Redevelopment Administration (ARA), the Bureau of Indian Affairs (BIA), and the Economic Development Administration (EDA) had succeeded in attracting 150 factories to reservations by 1972.

During 1957 to 1962, Indians formed a majority of the employees working in plants on the reservations. In the 1963 to 1969 period, however, somewhat less than half of all employees were Indians. Apparently this change came about for two reasons. First, in recent years many of the industrial plants were located just inside the reservation boundary and drew their labor force from both Indians residing on the reservation and non-Indians living off the reservation. Second, because of the high turnover and absenteeism of Indian employees, a few plants have found it necessary to reduce the number of Indians employed in order to stay in business.

The high turnover and absenteeism are largely due to the Indian's lack of experience with industrial discipline and work skills. These problems might be overcome by employing a program that combines counseling and basic education with on-the-job training in work skills. (Such an approach has been used to overcome similar obstacles in hiring, training, and retraining the hard-core unemployed.) At present, after a businessman has built his plant on reservation land provided by an Indian tribe, the BIA subsidizes wages for on-the-job training, but it does not provide for the counseling and education of workers.

Obstacles to Economic Development

Certain barriers have retarded industrialization on Indian reservations. The first is the completely inadequate transportation system on most reservations. For most manufacturers, product transportation costs form a significant percentage of total costs. Thus, roads, railroads, and airstrips are important.

The BIA has responsibility for the maintenance and improvement of Indian reservation roads on 165 Indian reservations in twenty-three states. Because of limited funds, the level of expenditure for maintenance and improvement of reservation roads is low. The system is therefore inadequate.

The bureau maintains airstrips in fifty-five Indian communities. During the winter, only air transportation is available to many communities. The bureau claims that most of these airstrips are inadequate to serve the communities within aviation safety standards.

For those industries which must locate near their market, being on or near an Indian reservation will not be advantageous. First, the poverty of the Indian lowers the effective demand for all goods, even vital necessities. Second, the Indian population on most reservations is so scattered that, even if incomes and potentially effective demand were high, the poor road system would prevent the concentration of demand.

Reservation Indians are the most poorly educated minority group in the United States. The 1970 census showed that the median years of schooling for American Indians was 8.6 years. Although school attendance has increased greatly since World War II, only half the young people have been completing high school.

This means that industries which require employees with relatively high educational attainment (minimum of high school graduation) find it impossible to obtain suitable employees at a reservation location.

An extreme lack of semiskilled or skilled manpower exists on the reservations. Since the mid-fifties, the bureau has taught few vocational courses in reservation schools. Moreover, the lack of prior industrialization means that reservation Indians have not had the advantage of industry training or apprenticeship programs. In addition, since World War II there has been considerable migration from the reservations, principally of those who would be the most desirable employees in industry.

Solutions tested and found successful in other rural areas may therefore be inappropriate for the reservations. Still, certain basic needs can best be met by reservation development programs. These may be summarized as follows:

1. *Self-sustaining activities.* The need for self-sustaining activities is inherent in the economic development process, since it cannot be based on continuing support from outside sources. If economic development is to be effective, it must move in the direction of activities that are able to maintain production apart from outside subsidy. In other words, economic activities must be profitable. They must be planned so that eventually they will take in more money than they pay out. This does not preclude initial subsidies of varying magnitude, but such subsidies must be justified on the basis that they will eventually become unnecessary and the activity will be capable of sustaining itself.
2. *An adequate standard of living.* The economic development system sought for a reservation should eventually provide the members of the tribe with an adequate standard of living. No other sector of American society

Obstacles to Economic Development

has a greater claim on our economy and our government for assistance in attaining this. Something more than economic development assistance may be required to achieve such a goal for some tribes. But at least the economic development objective should have as its goal the production of sufficient goods and services so as to provide an adequate standard of living.

3. *Opportunities for self-development.* Individuals must have opportunities within the reservation system to challenge their talents and achieve individual goals. They should have additional opportunities, within the framework of the society and economy, to exercise maximum feasible freedom of choice in the pursuit of useful and rewarding occupations. Obviously, the current isolation of most reservations and the scale of their economies will severely limit such freedom for those who choose to remain on the reservations. Ideally, those who prefer to enjoy the unique advantages of the reservation culture should not, by virtue of that choice, be restricted to menial and unrewarding occupations.

4. *Indian self-determination.* We must accept the values of Indian traditions and culture and construct the economic development system so as to preserve and strengthen those values. Outsiders cannot define values for the tribes, nor can they determine when any particular activity is supportive, destructive, or neutral. There will undoubtedly be trade-offs between traditional values and opportunities for economic growth, and men will disagree on these difficult decisions. Any system for providing economic development assistance to Indian reservations should therefore provide for considerable input from a democratic decision-making process on the reservation level.

12

Indian Rights in Latin America

Dale W. Kietzman

The legal and social status of Indian peoples in Latin America reflects the nature of the conquest and of the conquering powers. Spain and Portugal carried to the New World an extension of the feudal and hierarchical system of the Iberian peninsula. The Indians became serfs to the landowning lords. Serfs neither own land nor have been deprived of their lands; they pertain to the land.

At the time of the conquest, the Indians generally were presented with a single option: they could become Christians or suffer death. But becoming Christians did not modify their status at the lowest end of the feudal social scale. They still pertained to the land and were subject to work levies as determined by the landowner.

Only in Brazil was there any recognition of Indian tribes as sovereign nations. This principle was first stated in 1822 by José Bonifacio, the intellectual father of Brazilian independence. He wanted Indians to receive "justice, tolerance and consistency, with no restrictions on commercial transactions or intermarriage." His policy to "protect and integrate" was not put into practice until the founding of the Brazilian Indian Service by Marshal Rondon in 1910. In order to "protect" them, Brazilian constitutions since 1889 have made Indians who lived as Indians, that is, those still in their tribal groups, wards of the state.

In Spanish-speaking countries, the Indians were citizens, although of the lowest class. They were deprived, as are all economically and educationally disadvantaged citizens, of most of the privileges of citizenship. But in the general social upheavals both leading up to and following independence from Spain, the Indians had an opportunity, which some seized, to assert their position. But they have a long way to go, as the following brief survey indicates.

Each nation in Latin America presents a different history and therefore a different current manner of handling Indian affairs. Below are a limited number of examples, which will serve to characterize the variety of situations found. All facts and quotations come from official reports and publications of the *Instituto Indigenista Interamericano,* the organ of the Organization of American States that coordinates and reports on Indian affairs in the hemisphere (including those of North America).

1. Bolivia represents a country in which Indian peoples total more than 50 percent of the population. Two language groups dominate: the Quechua and the Aymara. The Indianist movement in Bolivia, which began at the time the Chaco War (1931-35), destroyed the country's feudal structures. Indians organized the first farming union in Bolivia in 1937. By 1972, a national conference, which clearly identified rural problems with Indian problems, declared that "national policies and problems cannot be separated from Indian policies and problems, because the nation is so distinctly rural." This is a factual

Indian Rights in Latin America

statement, but it does not reflect the social gap that separates the rural (Indian) masses from urban (largely non-Indian) developments.

2. Ecuador also has a 50 percent Indian population. The feudal structures have yet to be seriously challenged. While there has been a great deal of interest and activity on behalf of the Indians, there has never been a significant change in their status. Perhaps this summary paragraph in a report on Indianist activity in Ecuador explains why:

> *The Most Important Efforts:* In the most recent period, various efforts on behalf of the Indian population have been made. Unfortunately, these efforts have not been maintained long enough to have the desired effect; on other occasions, the programs have not been soundly structured on scientific principles; nor have proper techniques and methodologies been applied consistently; and at times, forces and factors have not permitted change in the Indian situation, because of the desires of those who benefit from the status quo.

3. Mexico has a significant Indian population, numbering approximately four million. These people speak at least two hundred different languages (the state of Oaxaca has the greatest linguistic diversity in this hemisphere) and are scattered through thousands of mountain valleys and villages. Indians have played a prominent part in shaping modern Mexico, and Mexico is the focus of *indigenismo* (Indianism), the identification of Indian values in national life. Mexico does not generally segregate Indian communities in terms of economic and political decisions, although some specialized educational programs have been developed. But the Indians who maintain traditional ways are at a distinct disadvan-

tage in the social and economic system. The price of upward mobility is still the loss of tribal ways.

4. Venezuela represents those countries with scattered Indian tribes. As in similar Spanish-speaking countries, little was done for these tribes until about 1950, and then, it was principally as a result of the prodding of *indigenistas* (Indianists) from Mexico. Typical of certain countries, Indian affairs are linked with the administration of religious groups under the Justice Ministry, which has caused considerable difficulty for Protestant missionary efforts. The actual assistance being given to Indian groups is minimal.

5. Brazil, of all Latin American countries, most nearly follows United States patterns. Theoretically, at least, the tribes are to be dealt with as sovereign groups. Reservation lands are assigned, and these lands are held in trust for the Indians by the National Indian Foundation (FUNAI). FUNAI also administers Indian programs under the Interior Ministry. In addition to health and self-help programs, attempts are made to provide basic education "appropriate to the Indian in view of his progressive integration into national society without loss of his cultural patterns and without abrupt changes." The last phrase is always interpreted to except those changes demanded by national development, such as the current program of highway construction throughout the Amazon Basin.

6. A unique national solution to the Indian problem is found in Paraguay. There the Guarani Indian language is considered a national language and is used as the medium of instruction and commerce, even in the capital city. Laws are written in Guarani, and distinctive national origins in the Guarani people are extolled. This very

healthy attitude does not carry over to some small, non-Guarani tribal groups in Paraguay, who receive practically no attention from the government. Fortunately Paraguay has permitted missions and the Mennonite colonies a reasonably free hand in giving assistance to these groups.

The situation of Native Americans in Latin America—politically, socially, educationally, and economically—is much more complex and, by that very factor, more difficult and more discouraging than in North America. The problems native peoples have encountered in the United States are magnified in Latin America by the multiplicity of governments, the instability of some of these governments, and by the isolation, and even intratribal divisions, imposed by national boundaries.

Yet the solution for their problems will be the same as in this country: the "healing of the nations" provided by Jesus Christ (Rev 22: 2).

13

Legitimate Political Aspirations

Charles E. Smith

The American Indian who knows Jesus Christ as Saviour and Lord has two very important reasons to be concerned with politics. First, God's love for the world includes government. Second, the needs of Indian people are very real, and many can be met through government action.

Historically, Christian missionary efforts have been focused upon bringing individuals to salvation in Christ or in gaining members for the various denominations. Rarely has the effort been made to disciple the whole man in accordance with the Great Commission given by Jesus Christ (Matt 28:19-20). For too long Christians have considered education, vocational training, home economics, and technical skill instruction less important than such "spiritual items" as church attendance.

Discipling a man surely would include equipping him to be a participant in the larger society. Jewish Christians of the first century were members of their Roman-dominated society without giving up their Jewish distinctives. Christian Indians, it would seem, can be an integral part of the dominant society without compromise to their Christianity or to their Indian traditions.

I have encountered at least six different objections to Christian Indian political involvement, each with scriptural proof texts:

1. The world is evil, and Christians must refrain from contact with it as much as possible (John 15:19).
2. The believer's sole responsibility is to win men to Christ (Prov 11: 30).
3. The believer should not allow politics and worldly cares to distract from his own spiritual calling (Matt 6: 33).
4. God is in control and does not need man's help (2 Chron 32: 8).
5. Politics is dirty and is therefore to be avoided. Even at its best, politics means compromise, and for Christians this is not permitted (2 Cor 6:17).
6. Political involvement does not make any difference anyway (John 18: 36).

These arguments for noninvolvement, as good as they may sound at first reading, are inadequate rationalizations and must be recognized as such. If concerned Christian Indians probe more deeply into the problem, they soon see the shallowness of this sort of head-in-the-sand thinking. Let us examine briefly each of the six arguments in the light of God's Word, history, and political reality.

The world may be tainted by sin, but God is still God, and the world belongs to Him. The greatest truth is that He gave His Son for the world (John 3:16). He has commanded Christians to bear witness in all parts of the world (Acts 1: 8). Christians are obligated to minister to the whole man, meeting both his spiritual and material needs. The disciple who gives a cup of water to a needy person will not go unrewarded (Matt 10: 42). On a number of occasions, Jesus

Legitimate Political Aspirations

reproved the Pharisees, the legalists of His day, for their shortcomings in this regard (Matt 12: 1-13; Luke 14: 1-4). If Christians love their neighbors as themselves, they cannot and will not place politics and religion in two different spheres.

Spiritual vitality, rather than being retarded by involvement in the world, is strengthened. How much is an individual life strengthened by seeing others moved by a word of encouragement? How shall the world know its great need apart from the contrast of Christian living?

Should Christians retire to the sideline, as the fourth argument suggests? Who will enter the Kingdom of heaven? Jesus' answer is not the man who piously mouths, "Lord, Lord," but he who does the will of the Father (Matt 7: 21). James specifies that believers must be "doers of the word, and not hearers only" (James 1: 22).

The argument that "politics is dirty" smacks of irresponsibility. Senator Mark O. Hatfield says that the decision of good, honest people to avoid politics "creates a serious vacuum of morality in places of public leadership."

Finally, the idea that it just doesn't make any difference is a cop-out on at least two levels. In the first place, it denies that God is interested in people, and, second, it fails to learn from history. Historically, God has worked through man. Small groups of men have had and continue to have great power to change operative structures, as Lenin has demonstrated in the Marxist revolution in this century.

I want to deal briefly with three questions in the context of Christian Indian leadership:

- What can I do to help my people?
- What can I aspire to?
- What hope is there for Indians as a people?

The two alternatives of either infiltrating the system or working outside it are both live options for the Indian Christian. Even as he chooses to infiltrate the system, the Christian concedes that, in all likelihood, the government is ungodly. But, like Joseph, Mordecai, and Daniel, the Indian *can* influence it through participation at key levels. This approach demands excellence, determination, and spiritual vitality.

To begin with, Christian Indians must learn how the system works and how to work within it. At the heart of American politics is the precinct, and it is at this level that the Indian must start. Party committees of local origin have power far exceeding their numbers. Too often positions go to less capable people by default.

Elected political offices will go to persons who have:

- A broad, deep understanding of people represented
- The ability to stand up and give verbal expression to their reasons, logic, and concern
- Organized their support by learning how to understand and meet the concerns of the electorate
- Demonstrated moral character, compassion, and leadership
- The self-confidence to expose themselves to criticism

The higher the elected position, the greater the need for breadth and depth of understanding. Running as an Indian candidate will be of greater value when the registration is heavily Indian. Where the Christian Indian, because of his heritage and his faith, runs as a minority candidate, he stands upon his record.

Obviously, an alternative way to infiltrate the system, other than through elections, is by being employed at the decision-making level. A Christian Indian, acting upon his

Legitimate Political Aspirations 109

values as a Christian and within the cultural heritage of being Indian, can be as fine a public official as can be found for any position within the governmental framework.

Working outside the system, the prophets of old greatly influenced the government of their times. Micah, Amos, Jeremiah, and Isaiah carried tremendous influence. Indians are being heard today. Witness the news coverage on Wounded Knee. Where is the Christian Indian who will be heard from on the political front? The dignity of a people needs to be thundered across America.

To what offices can the Christian Indian aspire? School boards, city councils, and state legislatures all have elected Indians and Christians in office. Why is there not currently an Indian in the Congress? The answer is twofold. First, not enough Indians are working at the grass roots of party politics. Like the old baseball farm system, so it is with major party candidates. You work your way up the system. With the exception of hero types (John Glenn) or supersuccessful types (Charles Percy), men work their way up the chairs (Mark Hatfield).

A second factor that could limit an Indian candidate is to be *only* an Indian candidate. The hard facts are that the states with the highest percentage of Indian population are: (1) Alaska, 17.05 percent; (2) New Mexico, 7.16 percent; (3) Arizona, 5.50 percent; (4) South Dakota, 4.86 percent; (5) Montana, 3.91 percent; (6) Oklahoma, 3.82 percent. To win, an Indian has to be a member of the choir (party) before he can be featured as a soloist (elected representative) on Indian grievances.

Having affirmed that a Christian Indian can aspire to the Congress of the United States, what is the holdup? A lack of verbal expressiveness hampers many Indian candidates. In an age where votes are captured as much by impressions as anything, effective verbal communication is a must. The press conferences, service clubs, campaign speeches, and personal conversations all lean heavily upon one's ability to give verbal expression. If one is to be elected, he must be good at verbal expression and thinking "off the cuff" with an accurate understanding of his position and facts.

Finally, there is the question of hope. Christians affirm that there is tremendous hope for the Indian people. Pragmatically, just getting Indian people together is a miracle-sized project. Reservation versus nonreservation or urban Indian, full blood versus mixed blood, and tribalism—these issues sharply divide the Indian population. Because of the sharpness of these divisions, only the spiritual oneness spoken of by Paul in Galatians 3:28 is the answer.

Education and employment also are key factors to be dealt with. To make it in the dominant society, Indians *must* compete. Granted, the dominant society has been and continues to be guilty of giving fish but seldom teaching Indians to fish. The non-Indian world has certainly been at fault, but the Indian is the one who continues to suffer. Christian Indians need to rise and lead in areas of political and social concern.

The question facing Christian Indians is: Are we preparing men to serve our people in all areas of life?

Appendix

FACTS ABOUT INDIANS IN AMERICA TODAY

Population Characteristics of the American Indian Today

The Indian population of the United States increased from about 500,000 in 1960 to 763,594 in 1970.[1] There are Indians in every state and the District of Columbia, but only eighteen states have significant populations in excess of 10,000 (See Table I).

Despite this population increase of 38 percent in the past decade, Indians represent the smallest of the three major ethnic minorities in the United States. In 1970, people of Spanish language background, numbering slightly over 9 million, constituted 4.5 percent of the United States population; and Blacks, some 22.5 million, represented 11 percent of the total population. This contrasts with less than 1 percent for the American Indian.

The median age of the Indian population today is 20.4 years, slightly above the 1960 median of 19.2 years. The median age of the Spanish language group was 20.7 years in 1970, and that of the Black population was 22.4 years, all

---

1. This figure does not include about thirty-five thousand Eskimo and Aleuts in Alaska, who, along with Indians, are collectively called Alaskan Natives in programs affecting that state.

of these far below the United States median of 28.1 years. This low median age for the Indian population is another indicator that it is a rapidly growing population.

The American Indians were the only ethnic group in the United States still classified as predominantly rural in 1970, with 55.4 percent of the total population scattered in rural areas. This represented a decrease from 70 percent of Indians living in rural areas in 1960, a trend which, however, paralleled that of the general United States population.

The Indian urban population totaled about 340,000 in 1970, up from 166,000 in 1960. In other words, the Indian urban population more than doubled in a single decade.

California had the largest number of urban Indians with 67,000; Oklahoma was next with 48,000. The Los Angeles urbanized area had the largest single concentration of Indians, with some 28,000 in 1970. Other cities with at least 10,000 Indians are New York, San Francisco, Oakland, and Oklahoma City. The Los Angeles area has drawn Indians from many places, but the tribes most heavily represented are the Navajo, other southwestern tribes, and the Cherokee. In Minneapolis and St. Paul, the migrants are mostly from the Chippewa and Sioux tribes; in Baltimore, they are Lumbee Indians; and in New York, they are Mohawks.

Migration from farm areas into the cities has been most substantial in the upper Midwest, where it is estimated that more than 50 percent of the Indians reaching age twenty have left rural areas in favor of the city. This contrasts with a net rural-to-urban migration of young people of only about 16 percent in Washington and Oregon. Thus, there is considerable variation in the migration pattern from tribe to tribe or region to region.

Presumably many Indians migrate in the hope of better-

Appendix

ing economic conditions. About 33 percent of Indian families had incomes below the poverty level, compared with 11 percent for the total United States population. About 20 percent of urban Indian families had incomes below the poverty level in 1969; the proportion was more than twice that high among rural Indian families. Although this would seem to indicate some betterment of economic position by moving to the city, limited job opportunities and relatively poor education offer little opportunity for rising above the poverty level, even after such a move.

Although there has been improvement in Indian education in recent decades, Indians 25 years old and over are still more than two years behind the United States population in median years of school completed. The national median is 12.1 years; for Indians it is 9.8. Furthermore, in 1970, 12 percent of Indians in rural areas had received no schooling at all, in contrast with less than 2 percent in the total United States rural population.

Although government and tribal programs have made marked progress in many aspects of American Indian life, Indians still start life from a level of extreme disadvantage. Improvements in income, employment, education, health, and housing still leave Indians far behind other Americans. Among rural Indians, the situation is even more serious. Income is generally lower, poverty deeper, education more limited, health poorer, and housing more inadequate than for the total United States rural population.

In addition, American Indians bear psychological problems engendered by a minority group position in the society as well as by the uncertainties of cultural transition. Moving quite rapidly from a rural to an urban situation involves many difficult adjustments. And until the larger problem of acculturation as opposed to separatism, or some middle ground between the two, is resolved, there will be anxiety on the part of the minority about its role and potential in a modern urbanized economy.

The American Indians also have both an economic and a cultural handicap in facing the current transitional phase involved in the policy which the Bureau of Indian Affairs is terming "self-determination without termination." This program aims to give them greater participation in planning and carrying out programs affecting their lives and culture, without termination of the unique trust relationship between Indians and the federal government.

A period of change can also be a period of opportunity. But when a cultural group is disadvantaged economically and socially, and is in a minority position in the surrounding society, the adjustments required to achieve meaningful change are especially trying.

Table I
Indian Population 1970—Urban and Rural Residence

	Total	Urban	Rural Nonfarm	Rural Farm
NORTHEAST				
Maine	1,872	856	1,001	15
New Hampshire	310	159	146	5
Vermont	204	15	166	23
Massachusetts	4,237	3,346	866	5
Rhode Island	1,417	1,224	188	5
Connecticut	3,322	1,859	453	10
New York	25,560	17,161	8,165	234
New Jersey	4,255	3,776	456	23
Pennsylvania	5,543	4,412	1,103	28
NORTH CENTRAL				
Ohio	6,181	5,079	976	126
Indiana	3,305	2,336	874	95
Illinois	10,304	9,542	687	75
Michigan	16,012	10,541	5,183	288
Wisconsin	18,776	7,439	10,963	374

Appendix

Minnesota	22,322	11,703	9,789	830
Iowa	2,924	2,052	784	88
Missouri	4,890	3,617	1,122	151
North Dakota	13,565	1,810	10,642	1,113
South Dakota	31,043	9,115	18,597	3,331
Nebraska	6,671	3,232	3,018	421
Kansas	8,261	6,130	1,814	317
SOUTH				
Delaware	479	180	285	14
Maryland	3,886	3,282	593	11
District of Columbia	673	673	—	—
Virginia	4,862	3,055	1,641	166
West Virginia	518	193	320	5
North Carolina	44,195	6,194	28,748	9,253
South Carolina	2,091	858	1,194	39
Georgia	2,271	1,579	637	55
Florida	6,392	4,275	1,961	156
Kentucky	1,322	934	364	24
Tennessee	1,432	1,095	324	13
Alabama	2,163	1,210	810	143
Mississippi	3,791	578	2,933	280
Arkansas	2,088	1,225	753	110
Louisiana	4,519	1,543	2,716	260
Oklahoma	96,803	47,623	44,019	5,161
Texas	16,921	14,567	2,126	228
WEST				
Montana	26,385	5,070	18,215	3,100
Idaho	6,646	1,990	3,500	1,156
Wyoming	4,717	1,040	2,938	739
Colorado	8,002	5,421	2,196	385
New Mexico	71,582	13,405	51,466	6,711
Arizona	94,310	16,442	70,808	7,060
Utah	10,551	3,689	5,606	1,256
Nevada	7,476	2,832	3,943	701
Washington	30,824	16,102	13,541	1,181
Oregon	13,210	6,976	5,705	529
California	88,263	67,202	19,955	1,106
Alaska	16,080	4,696	11,378	6
Hawaii	1,168	1,034	134	—
UNITED STATES	763,594	340,367	375,822	47,405

Indian Leadership Today

The success of past missionary work must be judged by the mature Indian leadership it has produced for today and is producing for tomorrow. It is God's plan that His church among Native Americans be built of Native American believers who display in themselves all the gifts needed for the growth of the Body of Christ.

Indian leadership is being felt in many secular disciplines, both within and outside the Indian community. Within the church, the promise of native leadership of a generation ago seems to be fading. Many United States denominations report a gradual advance in the average age of Native American pastors, with few young people preparing for Christian work.

This phenomenon may be due, in part, to an economic reality. The United States Bureau of Indian Affairs has now developed extensive incentives for training in secular careers, but none in areas of theology and Christian education. It is natural, therefore, that the number of Native Americans taking advantage of these secular educational opportunities should increase, seemingly at the expense of the sort of trained leadership the church might expect.

This does not mean that a strong, well-educated Christian leadership is not appearing within the Indian church. Just the opposite is true. Christian Indians are taking marked leadership in many areas. For example:

Leroy Falling, a Cherokee Indian who coordinates the higher education programs of the BIA, is an outstanding lay leader in the Church of God, Anderson, Indiana.

The secretary of Christian Hope Indian Eskimo Fellowship (CHIEF) is Kogee Thomas, a Creek/Seminole Indian

Appendix

who is now assistant dean of the University of California-Irvine. She serves on the coordinators committee for the State of California International Women's Year 1977; and on the executive committee of the United States American Indian Youth Council for Program and Implementation 1977-78. She has included in her career the editorship of the *American Indian Culture & Research Journal.* Miss Thomas was formerly associate and acting director of the American Indian Studies Center, University of California, Los Angeles.

At the 1976 conference of the National Indian Education Association in Albuquerque, a sizable percentage of the educators present identified themselves as Christians, and there was strong encouragement to organize as Indian Christian teachers.

As noted by Ray Baines in his article on education, the presence of this highly trained younger generation, many with college and graduate degrees, presents a serious problem for the Native American pastor, who typically has had fewer years of formal education. Unfortunately, as yet there is no seminary or seminary program designed for Native Americans, nor are scholarships readily available for study on this level.

Dr. Taylor McKenzie, a Navajo Indian and an outstanding Christian layman, is heading the development of an Indian medical school in Arizona. He is dean of the new school to open in the fall of 1977, and director of the Navajo Health Authority.

Although a number of colleges and universities in the eastern United States had the original purpose of offering Christian education to Indian students, only Bacone College in Muskogee, Oklahoma, continues in this tradition. This American Baptist institution, headed by Dr. Charles D. Holleyman, a Creek Indian, provides a campus atmosphere and curriculum in which Indian young people can feel at home.

The shortage of Native American pastors is met, in part, by a growing group of Indian evangelists and Bible teachers active in both the United States and Canada. While many pastors also occasionally devote time to conference work, the following prominent leaders give full time to this sort of work.

Tom Claus of Phoenix, Arizona, is a Mohawk Indian born near Brantford, Ontario. He has traveled throughout North, Central, and South America for more than thirty years, both as a part of a family singing group and as an effective evangelist. He founded the American Indian Crusade, which has sponsored an Indian ministry on over 150 reservations in North America.

Allen Earley, an Apache Indian from San Carlos, Arizona, is an American Indian Crusade evangelist trained at the Southwestern School of Missions in Flagstaff, Arizona. His life story, portrayed in the film *Apache Fire,* has increased the scope of his ministry.

Don Rovie, a Pima Indian from Clarksdale, Arizona, is sponsored by the United Indian Mission. A graduate of Biola College, he has traveled extensively and been greatly used by the Lord.

Tommy Francis, a Cree Indian from Prince Albert, Saskatchewan, is secretary of the Native Evangelical Fellowship of Canada. He graduated from Mo-Kah-Um Indian Bible School, Cass Lake, Minnesota. God has used his ministry across Canada.

Ken Antone, an Oneida Indian originally from near London, Ontario, who now resides in Oklahoma City, travels

Appendix

throughout North America with his singing family. They are well received by Indians everywhere.

Another widely known singing family is that of Ray Smith, a Chippewa Indian from Cass Lake, Minnesota. His ministry is under the auspices of the Christian and Missionary Alliance.

The Native American church now has available a large number of training institutes, most of them mission-sponsored, but with capable Indian teachers. These institutes, which generally lack accreditation, accept students with widely varying educational backgrounds. Their goal is to provide basic instruction in Christian subjects in order to prepare individuals for effective contributions as lay people in their local churches. The most prominent include:

American Indian Bible Institute, Norwalk, California
American Indian Bible Institute, Phoenix, Arizona
Brainerd Indian Training School, Hot Springs, South Dakota
Cook's Christian Training School, Phoenix, Arizona
Good Shepherd Bible School, Mobridge, South Dakota
Indian Bible Schools, sponsored by the Northern Canada Evangelical Mission in Round Lake, Ontario; by the Mennonites in Red Lake, Ontario; and by the Nazarene Church in Albuquerque, New Mexico
Keywatin Bible Institute, Lac La Birch, Alberta
Mo-Kah-Um Indian Bible School, Cass Lake, Minnesota
Mt. Echo Bible Institute, Great Valley, New York
Native Bible Institute, Palmer, Alaska
Native Bible Institute, Quesnel, British Columbia
Navajo Bible School, Window Rock, Arizona
Northwestern Bible School, Alberton, Montana
Southwestern School of Missions, Flagstaff, Arizona

The current leadership problem has been one of the felt needs which led to the creation of CHIEF (Christian Hope Indian Eskimo Fellowship). Its program includes leadership training seminars for pastors and mature laymen; a scholarship and educational information program for young people interested in preparing for Christian service; and an active exploration of the possibility of creating a Native American theological seminary.

Postscript

Conference on Indian Evangelism and Christian Leadership

RESOLUTION

RESOLVED THAT We, the delegates to the Conference on Indian Evangelism and Christian Leadership, call for a continuation of the evangelical fellowship we have found here.

We seek a vehicle by which we can express the spiritual bond which unites all evangelical believers among native American groups. We affirm that we are one in the Spirit; we are one in His love; we are one in the fellowship of the family of God.

We seek a vehicle of fellowship and of communication. We sense the great strength and diverse gifts and experiences of our fellow believers, and want to give to others, and receive from others that which God has taught each of us.

We sense the need for a strengthened and sharpened evangelical witness; for a growing and vigorous lay leadership; for greater educational and economic opportunities for our peoples; for vital Christian alternatives for our youth; for increased pride in our cultural heritage and in our race.

We believe we can best achieve these goals as we stand together as native Americans within the family of God.

As we become strong, and learn how to express our unity, we believe that this evangelical fellowship of native Christians will be heard in a powerful way by the Church at large, and will provide the moral foundations for evangelical witness and participation in all aspects of life in the dominant society.

To continue our fellowship, we commission an organizing committee to function on our behalf to bring into being a permanent vehicle for communication and fellowship among us. The committee shall operate within the following guidelines:

1. The committee shall be composed of nine persons, two-thirds of whom shall be Indian. The members should be drawn principally from the Southwest, for ease and economy in arranging committee sessions.
2. The committee is to report periodically in writing to the delegates present at this convention, who shall have the right to respond with their own thinking on any area of the committee's assignment.
3. In addition to working toward a permanent membership organization, the committee is also asked to arrange for a larger conference of native Americans, perhaps including sizable international delegations, to be held at a time and place determined by the committee.
4. Further program development, such as a research center or library, scholarship and extension seminar programs, shall be developed only as satisfactory progress is achieved toward incorporation, and as plans are developed that can be reviewed by the delegates to this con-

ference, with the understanding that great care will be exercised to guard the essential character of the new organization as a fellowship and communications vehicle among native American Christians.